THE OPENING YOUR HEART SERIES

Beloved: *Opening Your Heart, Part I,* is a six-lesson Bible study that lays a strong foundation for our true identity as beloved daughters of God.

Unshaken: *Opening Your Heart, Part II,* is a six-lesson Bible study that fills our spiritual toolbox with exactly what we need to grow stronger in our faith.

Steadfast: *Opening Your Heart, Part III,* a six-lesson Bible study, unpacks why we are hustling for our worth and how to conquer our fears.

THE KEEPING IN BALANCE SERIES

Harmony: Keeping in Balance, Part I
Perspective: Keeping in Balance, Part II
Exhale: Keeping in Balance, Part III

THE DISCOVERING OUR DIGNITY SERIES

Tapestry: Discovering Our Dignity, Part I
Legacy: Discovering our Dignity, Part II
Heritage: Discovering Our Dignity, Part III

For more information on all Walking with Purpose Bible studies please visit us at
walkingwithpurpose.com

walking with purpose

walking with purpose

Dear Friend,

Welcome to *Unshaken,* part II of the *Opening Your Heart* young adult Bible study series! You are about to begin an exciting journey closer to the heart of God. You can come as you are—with your questions, doubts, joys, and hopes.

You belong to a unique, world-changing generation. The way in which you are engaging and restoring culture brings hope and healing. You see the brokenness around you, and aren't content to just talk about solutions. But when you step out to create change, you will inevitably come under fire. There will be times when you will feel buried by fear of failure, and will worry that you don't measure up. This comes with the territory of stepping out and risking greatness. Two of the lies that the enemy loves to speak to a young woman when she sets out to be a difference maker are "it's all up to you," and "you are all alone." Delving into Scripture helps quiet the lies and draws you to truth. The truth is, God will do the work *in* and *through* you, and you are never alone. You are a part of a family, and all the saints in heaven are cheering for you as you run your race. "Therefore, since we are surrounded by such a great cloud of witnesses, let us throw off everything that hinders and the sin that so easily entangles. And let us run with perseverance the race marked out for us" (Hebrews 12:1).

If you had the chance to do the Bible study, *Beloved* (part I in the Opening Your Heart series), then you laid a foundation in terms of your true identity, how to have a personal relationship with Jesus, why and how to pray, the difference the Holy Spirit makes, how God the Father is everything you've ever hoped for, and more. *Unshaken* picks up where *Beloved* left off, introducing you to relationships, sacraments and truths that you'll want to understand and embrace each and every day. A spiritual foundation is laid out for you that gives your feet a firm place to land.

God doesn't want you spinning through life— untethered, wondering if what you are doing matters, if you matter, if you belong. With a passion that took Him to the cross, He wants you to know that you are adored and wanted, and that He has a plan for you. These truths will make more and more sense as you saturate your mind and heart in Scripture. So that's exactly what we're going to do as we journey through *Unshaken.*

My prayer is that you would grasp hold of this opportunity for a fresh start— that you would see yourself through the eyes of God, knowing that "whoever is in Christ is a new creation: the old things have passed away; behold, new things have come." 2 Cor. 5:17

God is doing a new thing in you, and I'm so excited to be with you on that journey~

Lisa Brenninkmeyer
Founder and Chief Purpose Officer, Walking with Purpose

Unshaken
Opening Your Heart Series
Part II

www.walkingwithpurpose.com

Authored by Lisa Brenninkmeyer
Cover and page design by True Cotton
Production management by Christine Welsko

IMPRIMATUR   + William E. Lori, S.T.D., Archbishop of Baltimore

Printed: January 2018

ISBN: 978-1-943173-12-9

Unshaken: *Opening Your Heart* Series, Part II

TABLE OF CONTENTS

INTRODUCTION

LESSONS

APPENDICES

ANSWER KEY

PRAYER PAGES

Welcome to Walking with Purpose

You have many choices when it comes to how you spend your time—thank you for choosing Walking with Purpose. Studying God's Word with an open and receptive heart will bring spiritual growth and enrichment to all aspects of your life, making every moment that you've invested well worth it.

Each one of us comes to this material from our own unique vantage point. You are welcome as you are. No previous experience is necessary. Some of you will find that the questions in this study cause you to think about concepts that are new to you. Others might find much is a review. God meets each one of us where we are, and He is always faithful, taking us to a deeper, better place spiritually, regardless of where we begin.

The Structure of *Opening Your Heart* Series

The *Opening Your Heart* series is a three-part Bible study, each of which can stand alone, or all three can be completed one after the other. Each six-week Bible study integrates Scripture with the teachings of the Roman Catholic Church to point us to principles that help us manage life's pace and pressure while living with calm and steadiness.

This Bible study can be used on your own, giving you great material for daily Scripture meditation and prayer. It also lends itself well to group discussion. We encourage you to gather your tribe—a handful of friends who want more out of their spiritual lives. The accountability and deeper friendship that will result make it so much easier to live out the truths contained in these pages.

Study Guide Format and Reference Materials

Each of the three parts of *Opening Your Heart* is divided into three sections:

The first section comprises six lessons, which are divided into five "days" to help you form a habit of reading and reflecting on God's Word regularly. If you are a young woman who has only bits and pieces of time throughout your day to accomplish tasks, you will find this breakdown of the lessons especially helpful. Each day focuses on Scripture readings and related teaching passages, and ends with a Quiet Your Heart reflection, which should lead you to a time of personal prayer. In addition, Day Five includes a Saint's Story; a lesson conclusion; a resolution section, in which you set a goal for yourself based on a theme of the lesson; and short clips from the *Catechism of the Catholic Church*, which are referenced throughout the lesson to complement the Scripture study.

The second section, the appendices, contains supplemental materials referred to during the study.

The third section contains the answer key. You will benefit so much more from the course study if you work through the questions on your own, searching your heart, as this is your very personal journey of faith. The answer key is meant to enhance small group discussion and provide personal guidance or insight when needed.

A memory verse has been chosen for each part of the *Opening Your Heart* series, and we encourage you to memorize each of them as you move through the course. An illustration of the Bible verse can be found at the back of the Bible study, and color versions and phone lock screens can be downloaded from our website.

At the end of the book are pages on which to write weekly prayer intentions.

The Bible
The recommended Bible translations for use in Walking with Purpose studies are: The New American Bible, which is the translation used in the United States for the readings at Mass; The Revised Standard Version, Catholic Edition; and The Jerusalem Bible.

Walking with Purpose™ Young Adult Bible Studies

The *Opening Your Heart* Series

Beloved: *Opening Your Heart, Part I* is a six-lesson Bible study that lays a strong foundation for our true identity as beloved daughters of God. We'll learn that we belong to a family that will never abandon us. We'll encounter grace and practical tools to make God our first priority. Jesus will meet us personally in the pages of His Word, and we'll be transformed as a result.

Unshaken: *Opening Your Heart, Part II* is a six-lesson Bible study that fills our spiritual toolbox with exactly what we need to grow stronger in our faith and discover our vocations. We'll discuss why and how we should read the Bible, what difference the sacraments really make in our lives, and how to bravely face challenges in our efforts to follow Christ.

Steadfast: *Opening Your Heart, Part III,* a six-lesson Bible study, unpacks why we are hustling for our worth and how to conquer our fears. We'll look at the role of suffering and forgiveness in our lives, and dig deeper into how we can truly change in the areas where we have felt enslaved. We'll explore life purpose, our vocations, and the depth of God's personal love for His beloved children.

The *Keeping in Balance* Series: *Coming Soon*

Harmony: *Keeping in Balance, Part I* is a seven-lesson Bible study that helps us to get a grip on our lives by looking at the importance of authenticity, setting priorities, managing expectations, and having healthy relationships. We'll also explore finding a balance between mediocrity and perfectionism so that we can become the women God created us to be without stressing or striving.

Perspective: *Keeping in Balance, Part II* is a six-lesson Bible study that addresses how we can become more content, grow stronger in areas where we've failed a million times, and get moving when we feel like settling for the status quo. *Perspective* also explores how we can engage our culture as Catholics at a time when the reputation of Christians is at an all-time low.

Exhale: *Keeping in Balance, Part III* is a six-lesson Bible study that helps us establish a rhythm of rest, worship, and surrender. If you long for more simplicity in your life and are ready to order your thoughts so you can experience inner peace, this Bible study will both inspire you and provide you with practical steps to make positive changes.

The *Discovering Our Dignity* Series: *Coming Soon*

Tapestry: *Discovering Our Dignity, Part I* is a six-lesson Bible study that explores the beginning of salvation history through the eyes of the women of Genesis. The difficulties they struggled with are remarkably similar to our own: relationship challenges, the death of dreams, the lure of compromise, and the danger of self-reliance. We'll learn from their mistakes as we apply age-old wisdom to our modern challenges.

Legacy: *Discovering Our Dignity, Part II* is a nine-lesson Bible study that picks up where *Tapestry* left off. Our exploration of the women of salvation history continues as we move further into the Old Testament. We'll explore a myriad of women's issues such as loneliness, shame, leadership challenges, and making a difference in the world.

Heritage: *Discovering Our Dignity, Part III* is a seven-lesson Bible study that highlights key women of the New Testament. Mary and Martha will help us explore the balance of work and worship, and the poor widow will shed new light on what it means to live sacrifically. We'll be inspired especially by Mary, the Blessed Mother, as we apply her wisdom to our daily challenges.

Walking with Purpose™ Website

Please visit our website at www.walkingwithpurpose.com to find supplemental materials that complement our Bible studies; a link to our online store for additional Bible studies, DVDs, books, and more; and the following free content:

WWP Scripture Printables of our exclusively designed verse cards that complement all Bible studies. Available in various sizes, lock screens for phones, and a format that allows you to e-mail them to friends.

WWP Bible Study Playlists of Lisa's favorite music to accompany each Bible study.

WWP Videos of all Connect Coffee Talks by Lisa Brenninkmeyer.

WWP Blog by Lisa Brenninkmeyer, a safe place where you are welcome, where the mask can drop and you can be real. Subscribe for updates.

WWP Leadership Development Program

We are here to help you take your leadership to the next level! Through our training, you'll discover insights that help you achieve your leadership potential. You'll be empowered to step out of your comfort zone and experience the rush of serving God with passion and purpose. We want you to know that you are not alone; we offer you encouragement and the tools you need to reach out to a world that desperately needs to experience the love of God.

Links to WWP Social Media

Twitter, Pinterest, Facebook, Instagram

Walking with Purpose™ Mission Statement

Walking with Purpose aims to bring women to a deeper personal relationship with Jesus Christ by offering personal studies and small group discussions that link our everyday challenges and struggles with the solutions given to us through the teachings of Christ and the Roman Catholic Church.

About the Author

Lisa Brenninkmeyer, raised as an evangelical Protestant, entered the Catholic Church in 1991. She has led Bible studies in Europe, Mexico, and the United States, and has written curricula for women and children. She founded Walking with Purpose in 2008 out of a desire to see women come to know Christ personally. Her speaking and writing are inspired by a desire to see women transformed as they realize how much God loves them. She holds a BA in psychology from St. Olaf College. She lives with her husband, Leo, and their seven children in St. Augustine, Florida.

Lessons

Walking with Purpose is a community of women growing in faith – together! This is where women are gathering. Join us!

www.walkingwithpurpose.com/find-program-near

Lesson 1

FIGHT LIKE A GIRL ~ THE BATTLE IS REAL

Introduction

"I didn't go to religion to make me happy. I always knew a bottle of Port would do that. If you want a religion to make you feel really comfortable, I certainly don't recommend Christianity." —C. S. Lewis

There's nothing I'm more passionate about than seeing women come to know Jesus in a personal, life-changing way. Our time on earth is so short, and there's no more important decision than whether or not we'll follow Christ. The thought of women spending their whole lives looking in the wrong places for the only love and relationship that will *truly satisfy* totally wrecks me. Knowing that true freedom, fulfillment, and peace are available to them through Christ, and knowing that so many women have never heard the gospel explained in a way that they really understand . . . Well, sometimes I think I just can't bear it.

Because I desperately want women to just give faith in Christ a *try*, it can be really tempting to "sell" Jesus—to tell a would-be follower of Christ of all the perks of faith, leaving out any bits that might be off-putting. "He'll fill your emptiness! He'll give you peace in circumstances that you would never have thought you could endure! He'll restore what's broken! He'll never leave you!" Before you panic and think I'm going to make the point that all those things are false advertising, let me assure you, they are all *true*. They are promises that we can count on. But they aren't the whole story. And only talking about the sweet truths and never the more difficult ones is a bit like expecting a child to grow strong while only eating cake. Ultimately that would be a disservice. In order to grow strong, we need the "meat."

As we study Jesus in the Gospels, it's clear that there was nothing He wanted more than for people to follow Him. But at no point did He attempt to draw them closer by just giving them the comforting truths. In fact, when a large crowd gathered around Him, over and over again He would say the very things that caused people to walk away. Why? If He cared about their souls, wouldn't He have done anything to get them to stay?

Jesus let them choose. He never compromised or watered down truth to win them over. He didn't try to talk them into joining His club.

What was true then is true now. Jesus isn't interested in us giving Him a nod of approval, or just attending His weekly get-togethers, or wearing a label that has no bearing on our hearts. He wants us to be *all in*. He wants a wholehearted commitment from us. He wants to be the game changer that turns our world upside down. Because of this, following Christ can be hard. It's always costly. It involves challenges that aren't for the fainthearted. He leads us onto a spiritual battlefield where the fighting can be fierce and relentless.

You've got to eat well to be a strong fighter. This means we can't just gorge on sweets. We've got to tuck into some meat. This lesson challenges us to take a good and honest look at the level of commitment Jesus is asking from us. We're going to focus on the challenges instead of the perks. Why? Because when life gets hard (which it inevitably will or might even be in this very moment), I don't want you to feel sideswiped or to wonder if your tough circumstances mean that God doesn't love you. Following Christ means entering into a battle that requires courage and perseverance. It isn't easy. But it is so very worth it.

Day One
THE CHALLENGE TO DENY YOURSELF

1. What condition did Jesus give for following Him in Luke 9:23?

2. The alternative to denying yourself and following Christ is saying, "I'll follow Jesus when it's comfortable. But this area of my life is off-limits. When it comes to [blank], I'm doing it my way." Is there an area of your life where what Jesus is asking of you just seems too much? Where are you feeling tempted to take the easy way out?

3. Picking up a cross and carrying it is always painful. It involves accepting a load that God has asked you to carry, and *walking forward*. This is different from sitting down with the weight of the cross on your back, a pool of pity in the tears at your feet. Picking up a cross is accepting circumstances that you are powerless to change, and determining to allow them to refine you, to sharpen you, to make you more spiritually fit. What cross has God asked you to pick up and carry forward?

4. What do we gain if we are willing to "lose our lives" for the sake of Christ? See Luke 9:24.

Quiet your heart and enjoy His presence. . . . Are you willing to lose your life for His sake?

". . . he must deny himself and take up his cross daily . . ." (Luke 9:23)

Daily. As in, day after day. It's one thing to gear up for one really tough challenge and to give it all you've got. When we know something hard has a clear end point, we can hit the dig-deeper button and power through. But the self-sacrifice that Jesus asks of us is the kind that feels especially difficult because there is no guarantee that the end is in sight. We are to make a daily decision to deny ourselves, pick up our cross, and follow Jesus. "For whoever wishes to save his life will lose it, but whoever loses his life for [Jesus'] sake will save it" (Luke 9:24). Let's never forget the second part of that verse. The end of the story is not misery. The end of the story is life—a life well lived; a life with meaning; a life with depth. A life with empathy because you know—you understand. A life in which you have loved Jesus for who He is, not what He gives you. A life in which the message of Calvary has become your story: After death comes the promised resurrection.

Day Two
THE CHALLENGE TO ACCEPT HEALTHY CONFLICT

Read Matthew 10:34–39.

1. Did Jesus promise that following Him would make all our relationships peaceful and conflict-free? Have you experienced conflict in relationships as your values, morals, and goals have changed as a result of following Christ?

2. Did Jesus say in Matthew 10:37 that we aren't supposed to love our families? What important distinction is made in this verse regarding our love for others and our love for Christ?

We are called to be committed to our families and to love them as Christ loves us. But when we have to make a choice between pleasing God and pleasing the people in our lives (even those who are closest to us), we are to choose God. While Jesus did say, "blessed are the peacemakers" (Matthew 5:9), He never advocated the kind of peace that ignores or avoids hard discussions just for the sake of artificial harmony.

3. When we have chosen to follow Christ and people close to us are following a different path, conflict inevitably arises. Most people respond in one of two ways. They either avoid uncomfortable discussions or situations, and if that involves compromise at times, so be it. Or they are always willing to engage, but feedback from others would suggest that they are coming off as judgmental. *So what exactly are we supposed to do?* Oh, if only there was a manual to follow with a perfect response for every situation we might face. The Bible doesn't give us a concise answer to every sticky position we might find ourselves in, but it does provide principles that we can apply to a variety of circumstances. Read the following verses from Ephesians 4, noting the principles that we are to follow when we experience conflict with others because of our faith.

Ephesians 4:2

Ephesians 4:26

Ephesians 4:29

Ephesians 4:32

Quiet your heart and enjoy His presence. . . . He heals the brokenhearted and binds up their wounds (Psalm 147:3).

As Christians, we are called to be "imitators of God" (Ephesians 5:1). As we seek to reflect Him to a world that finds Him repugnant and divisive, there will be times when conflict arises. When it does, we aren't to shrink back and compromise. We aren't to deny what we know to be true. But as we communicate, we should be doing it in a way that makes it clear it's all about Him, not all about us. And perhaps that's where a lot of our difficulties lie. We take things personally. We get our feelings hurt. We feel devalued, alone, dismissed. These are genuine hurts, and the Lord does not take lightly the fact that you are suffering for Him. But He asks that you bring that hurt back to Him instead of responding in bitterness, rage, and anger. Those feelings have got to go somewhere. We can bury them, we can hurl them back at the people we disagree with, or we can take them to Jesus and ask Him to absorb them in His limitless love. Have you been hurt by people who don't respect or embrace your decision to follow Christ? Go to God with your pain. He listens and cares. He is waiting to bind up your wounds and kiss your tears.

Day Three
THE CHALLENGE TO STAND FIRM

1. What do Luke 22:31 and 1 Peter 5:8 reveal about the source of some of our challenges?

2. How is the whole of man's history described in CCC 409? Where do we find ourselves in the midst of this description?

3. As we engage in that battle, what does 1 Corinthians 16:13 call us to do? Can you apply that verse to a specific challenge in your life today?

As we face specific challenges, being watchful means being aware of times when the devil is at work, stirring up trouble and making things worse. We are wise to always remain aware of who the real enemy is. As we face these challenges, we need to stand firm. The devil wants to take us out at the knees, to see us give up. God calls us to stand firm in the face of this. He calls us to remain courageous and strong—not because we have confidence in our own strength, but because of our confidence in *Him*.

4. How do we stand firm in our faith, according to CCC 162?

Quiet your heart and enjoy His presence. . . . "the One who is in you is greater than he who is in the world" (1 John 4:4).

Do you know how terrified the enemy of your soul is of you?

You may think of him and the evil in the world as being powerful and pervasive, and you're right. He is powerful, and it is pervasive. But authority trumps power. What do I mean by that?

Think of a policeman directing traffic. An enormous Mack truck could be driving down that road, but if a policeman stepped into the road and held up his hand, that Mack truck would stop. Obviously, the truck driver wouldn't want to run over the policeman. But there is more at play here—it is also the authority of the policeman that causes the driver to stop. And you have access to the greatest authority in the universe because He is your daddy. And He loves you. And He steps out and fights for you.

If you can recognize who you are as a child of the King, if you know the truth of Scripture and have it at your fingertips, you can step into the spiritual battle with authority, and Satan will be terrified of you your every waking moment. Men and women who know who they are in Christ are his worst nightmare.

Spend some time meditating on God's authority and power. Thank Him for stepping out and fighting for you.

Day Four
THE CHALLENGE TO STAY CHILDLIKE

With all this focus on the things we need to do (deny ourselves, accept healthy conflict, stand firm), we can think it's all up to us. It's easy to lose sight of the *type* of faith that God wants us to cultivate.

1. Why does it matter if we remain childlike? See Matthew 18:2–4.

2. How would you describe the *opposite* of a childlike faith?

3. Childlike faith isn't naive; it's trusting of God. It isn't about being innocent; it's about being dependent. It's a steady acknowledgment that it isn't all up to us. What we can't do ourselves, Jesus will do. It's an acknowledgment that we aren't perfect supersaints, but are spiritual children who desperately need God. For people who like to be strong and self-sufficient, this is a challenge. In what area of your life do you find it most difficult to exhibit childlike faith?

4. Jesus offers to take up residence within us, but it's up to us to receive His presence as a gift. Read Appendix 2, "Conversion of Heart." Have you experienced conversion of heart? Journal your thoughts below.

Quiet your heart and enjoy His presence. . . . Come empty and ask Him to fill you.

It's a challenge to make sure our confidence is rooted in God and not in our own abilities and strength. Anytime we find ourselves white-knuckling it[1] in the spiritual battle, trying so hard to be perfect that we are worn out, we have forgotten the secret of the Christian life. What's that secret? God dwells within us through the Holy Spirit, and He wants to do the work in and through us. He wants us to live a life of constant dependence on His care and guidance. God knows that on our own, we are no match for the intensity of the spiritual battle. Anytime we fool ourselves into thinking that we're doing OK without Him, we are setting ourselves up for defeat. Our prayer life indicates just how much we are relying on Him.

As we set out to follow Christ, we need to be sure to meet the challenges in God's strength, not in our own.

"Not by might, not by power, but by my spirit, says the LORD *of hosts." (Zechariah 4:6)*

"Finally, be strong in the Lord and in the strength of HIS *might." (emphasis added) (Ephesians 6:10)*

Take some time to confess any tendency to rely on yourself instead of on God. Reaffirm your faith in His strength and power.

---

[1] "White-knuckling it" means that we're doing something in a state of fear and tension. It's a picture of clenching something so tightly that our knuckles turn white.

Day Five
SAINT'S STORY

Saint Perpetua and Saint Felicity

Often, we think of saints as those whose faithfulness and devotion were called upon to make the ultimate sacrifice. These saints followed Christ to the point of shedding blood. While not every story ends this way, it did for Perpetua and Felicity.

Perpetua was a Roman noblewoman blessed with beauty, wisdom, and high birth. But more than anything, she was a Christian. And when the time came to choose what defined her most deeply, she declared herself to be a Christian even unto death. Felicity was a slave whose devotion to the Lord and her mistress, Perpetua, led her to follow in Perpetua's footsteps completely.

From Perpetua's life, we learn that martyrdom is not a matter of a moment. It is the crowning second of many days of quiet faithfulness. It is one thing to be heroic in front of a crowded stadium chanting for blood, which eventually happened when she and Felicity faced the wild beasts while singing "Te Deum." But this was only the final chapter of many struggles and many battles. And you, too, have battles that you must fight in the solitude of your own heart, with God and the saints as your witnesses.

Our enemy in this world is not made of flesh and blood. Our battle is against the unseen powers that wage war against our spirits, inside our minds, and in our hearts. What are the enemies that range themselves against us? How are they to be conquered?

One of our greatest foes is fear. There is a fear that worms its way into a woman's heart; it is the devil's envoy, a parasite on God's blessings. Have you ever not trusted that God will take care of you and the ones you love? Have you ever failed to be faithful to God because you were anxious about what other people would think of you? Have you ever shied away from doing something for God or for others because you thought you were not capable, strong, or intelligent enough? Have you ever worried that Jesus might be disgusted with your weakness and your sins of pride and sensuality? Have you ever been tempted to give up and just let it all slide because you thought you could never win? These are your battles, but Jesus and the saints are all on your side, rooting for you, cheering for you, ready to help you at the slightest hint of a prayer.

So how will you conquer this fear? Listen to Saint John, who says, "Perfect love casts out all fear" (1 John 4:18). It is the love of God poured out into your heart that will give you the strength to tread on the serpent's head.

This was how Felicity and Perpetua conquered. Before they entered the arena, Perpetua had several dreams and visions of what would soon come to pass. She saw herself climbing up a ladder to heaven, carefully avoiding the weapons being thrust at them from all sides, and stepping over the head of the devil on her way up. She saw the saints in heaven calling them, cheering them on. In another dream, she saw herself as a gladiator doing battle with an Egyptian in a crowded amphitheater. And in these visions, Perpetua understood that her true enemy was not the wild beasts that were waiting for her in the arena, but the temptations that would dissuade her from her deepest identity as a Christian. Her heavenly reward was worth the trials of the world, but she knew that she and Felicity must resist the urge to shrink back in perceived safety, away from the Lord's call to battle.

We live in a time of intense spiritual warfare. These are times unlike any other, when the true Christians following in Jesus' way and living lives honoring God will give immense glory to Him. You are blessed; you are gifted with grace. And if God calls you to do battle against these spiritual foes, it is because He knows you can win. Remember the words of Saint Paul and tell yourself that no matter what challenges you face, "I can do all things through him who strengthens me" (Philippians 4:13).

As you read Saint Perpetua and Saint Felicity's story, do you recognize some spiritual foes they faced that you currently struggle with? What can you learn from these saints to help you be victorious in the battle?

Conclusion

"For our struggle is not with flesh and blood but with the principalities, with the powers, with the world rulers of this present darkness, with the evil spirits in the heavens." (Ephesians 6:12)

Most things that are really worthwhile involve some hard work, and the Christian life is no exception. If we choose to live above the level of mediocrity, then we will soon see that the Christian life is a battle, and in this battle, we have some enemies.

We need only look at Christ's words and actions to see that He believes in the existence of the devil (1 John 3:8; Matthew 4:1–11; Mark 1:21–27, 3:11–15, 5:1–20). We need to strike a balance between being aware of Satan's work in our world and giving him more attention than he deserves. C. S. Lewis stated it well when he wrote, "There are two equal and opposite errors into which our race can fall about the devils. One is to disbelieve in their existence. The other is to believe, and to feel an excessive and unhealthy interest in them."[2]

Satan is the tempter, and he tries to keep us from following Jesus in many ways. Like no other time in history, women have the capability to really make a difference in the world. Yet we can be quickly distracted by things that don't matter. These things seem very important in the moment, but if we were to take a step back and think about whether they matter eternally, we might choose to spend our time in different places. Satan tempts us—not to join him, but simply to do nothing, to watch from the sidelines.

When we sit on the sidelines, he's not nearly as interested in us. Why? We aren't getting in his way! We're not having a real effect on the battle. But when we step in and decide that we want to be women who bring change, who make this world a better place—this gets him annoyed. He knows the power of one person's holiness. So he gets out his weapons and makes it challenging to follow Christ and really make a difference in this world.

This reality may make you want to head over to the sidelines, where it seems safer. But if we do that, what will happen to our culture? What will happen to the many hearts that won't be touched by the love of Christ?

Jump into the battle. You'll never regret it, because it is there that you will experience God's great power. "The one who is in you [Christ] is greater than the one who is in the world [Satan]" (1 John 4:4). In this battle, there are no vacations. But this life of adventure is the only one truly worth living.

"Evil can only exist if good men do nothing." —Edmund Burke

My Resolution

In what specific way will I apply what I have learned in this lesson?

"My Resolution" is your opportunity to write down one specific personal application from this lesson. We can take in a lot of information from studying the Bible, but if

---

[2] C. S. Lewis, *The Screwtape Letters* (New York: Touchstone, 1996), 15.

we don't translate it into action, we have totally missed the point. In James 1:22, we're told that we shouldn't just hear the Word of God; we are to "do what it says." So what qualities should be found in a good resolution? It should be **personal** (use *I, me, my, mine*), it should be **possible** (don't choose something so far-fetched that you'll just become discouraged), it should be **measurable** (a specific goal to achieve within a specific time period), and it should be **action oriented** (not just a spiritual thought).

Examples:

1. I commit this week to living out my baptism to the utmost. When I feel discouragement or self-pity, I won't give in to it. Instead, I'll refocus on what I *can* do: love. Alone, I can do nothing. But with God, all things are possible.

2. I commit to becoming a woman of prayer. I recognize that I am in a battle, and there are no vacations. My greatest weapon is prayer—this unleashes God's power in my life. When I don't pray, I am saying that I can do it all on my own. This self-sufficiency will reduce the flow of grace into my life. Because I believe this, I am going to consistently pray for ten minutes each morning. I will recognize that the quantity of my prayers can sometimes be as important as the quality. I will honestly assess whether I am spending enough time with God to make a real impact on my life.

3. I commit this week to refrain from complaining about my challenges. When I stop focusing on my desire for comfort, I can see the value of challenges. They make me stronger as I exercise the muscles of my will. With each yes to God and each no to self, I am changed, and for the better. I commit this week to a change in attitude: no complaining.

My resolution:

Catechism Clips

CCC 162 Faith is an entirely free gift that God makes to man. We can lose this priceless gift, as St. Paul indicated to St. Timothy: "Wage the good warfare, holding faith and a good conscience. By rejecting conscience, certain persons have made shipwreck of their faith." To live, grow and persevere in the faith until the end we must nourish it with the word of God; we must beg the Lord to increase our faith; it must be "working through charity," abounding in hope, and rooted in the faith of the Church.

CCC 409 This dramatic situation of "the whole world [which] is in the power of the evil one" makes man's life a battle:

> The whole of man's history has been the story of dour combat with the powers of evil, stretching, so our Lord tells us, from the very dawn of history until the last day. Finding himself in the midst of the battlefield man has to struggle to do what is right, and it is at great cost to himself, and aided by God's grace, that he succeeds in achieving his own inner integrity.

Lesson 2

FILLED TO OVERFLOWING ~ WE NEED THE EUCHARIST

Introduction

Even though I didn't convert to Catholicism until I was an adult, I've enjoyed a close friendship with Christ since childhood. I knew He loved and cared about me personally. Turning to Him in prayer with my concerns and my joys was easy. I can't remember a time when I didn't love the Bible, when reading it daily wasn't just my habit, but my source of peace.

The sacraments are the normal means by which we receive God's grace, but the Catechism teaches us that God *can* and *does* work outside the sacraments. I know this to be true. My experience of God as a Protestant was real, and I felt satisfied. I was not longing for more. In truth, I had no idea there was anything more to long for, spiritually speaking. I had my Bible and my personal relationship with Jesus. It felt like enough.

I became Catholic in my early twenties, not because of a love for the sacraments, but because I was in love with a handsome Brit who happened to be Catholic. I wanted spiritual unity in our marriage, so I was willing to convert. Due to my ignorance (and a less than stellar RCIA experience), before my conversion the sacraments seemed like choices in the grocery store: If I wanted to take advantage of them, they were there. But if I felt satisfied with what I had, they could sit on the shelf. For years, that is where I left the Eucharist.

My journey toward discovering the riches of the sacraments began with a long period of frustration. I was trying so hard to figure everything out, reading book after book. I found I could be convinced by any number of different perspectives. "Which one is true?" I would ask God.

Through studying the Bible passages in which Jesus gives Peter the authority to lead the Church, I began to learn that God didn't want me to be confused about important matters of faith. He had entrusted the Catholic Church with the job of interpreting

Scripture and teaching Christ's followers. In the words of philosopher Peter Kreeft, "Scripture itself calls the Church 'the pillar and ground of the truth.' (1 Tim. 3:15) Scripture was the Church's textbook, but the Church was the living teacher who taught and interpreted that textbook."[3]

I could trust what the Church taught. This was groundbreaking information for me. I had never thought about Scripture in that way. But when I considered that the earliest Christians didn't have Bibles (they had to rely on the oral tradition of the Catholic Church), I had to let go of some previously held assumptions.

That being said, I still found it hard to believe in Christ's real presence in the Eucharist. I didn't understand it. I couldn't prove it. I couldn't explain it.

Hebrews 11:1 made a real impact on me at this time. It says, "Faith is the realization of what is hoped for and the evidence of things not seen." I grasped the fact that I was going to have to take a leap of faith. Until I stepped out and decided to believe that Christ was truly present in the Eucharist, I wasn't going to receive the benefits that He was offering. "Lord, I believe; help my disbelief," became my prayer. And this is a prayer He *loves* to answer.

I find it difficult to describe the difference this has made in my life. How can I put words to such intimacy, such depth of friendship, such a source of inner peace? When I receive Christ in the Eucharist, I receive strength and grace. Practically, this means that I can get things done for my family and for Christ that I wasn't previously able to do. I have experienced exponential growth, a supernatural stretching of my resources that leaves me amazed.

There are times people ask me how I "get it all done." They wonder how I can find enough time to write, and speak, and work within the ministry of Walking with Purpose while doing my best to meet the needs of my husband and seven children.

It's the *real presence* of Jesus. I am like a glove, sitting lifeless on a table. But when He fills me, He can do all sorts of things in spite of my limitations. I don't feel worthy of His presence within me, but I am so grateful that He makes Himself so available. He waits for me every day in the Eucharist. What a waste it would be if I left Him on the shelf. Today, I embrace Him whenever possible.

---

[3] Peter Kreeft, *Jesus Shock* (Singer Island, FL: Beacon Publishing, 2008), 113.

Day One
THIS ISN'T SOME NEW IDEA

The *Compendium of the Catechism of the Catholic Church* 282 states: "Jesus Christ is present in the Eucharist in a unique and incomparable way. He is present in a true, real, and substantial way, with his Body and his Blood, with his Soul and his Divinity. In the Eucharist, therefore, there is present in a sacramental way, that is, under the Eucharistic species of bread and wine, Christ whole and entire, God and Man."

Some of us read that and think to ourselves, "I know. This is what I've always been taught." Maybe you can even recite a memorized version of that truth.

Others read the very same thing and think, "*What?* Where did that come from?" They might not say it out loud, but it's what they are thinking. I know. It was my first reaction many years ago. When you haven't grown up being taught something, it's hard to let go of old beliefs and embrace a teaching that says bread and wine actually become Jesus—His body, blood, soul, and divinity. So for the sake of those of us who need a little background, let's head back to the Old Testament. God started dropping hints about the Eucharist to His people pretty early on.

For hundreds of years, God's people (the Israelites) had been enslaved by the Egyptians. God chose a man named Moses to be His mouthpiece and to lead His people to freedom. To convince Pharaoh that freeing the Israelites would be in his best interest, God sent ten plagues on Egypt. The final plague was the worst: Every firstborn—human and animal—would be killed. The Israelites would be protected from this plague as long as they followed God's instructions.

1. A. What instructions did God give the Israelites in order for them to escape the tenth plague? Read Exodus 12:3–8.

If the Israelites wanted to live, their doors needed to be covered by the blood of the lamb, and the Passover lamb needed to be eaten. This was called the Passover Ritual. God told the Israelites to remember that day forever and continue to celebrate it once every year.

B. How did John the Baptist refer to Jesus in John 1:29?

C. The last Passover Jesus celebrated with His disciples (commonly called the Lord's Supper) is described in Matthew 26:26–28. What did He give the disciples to eat at that meal, and what did He tell them it was?

2. After the tenth plague, Pharaoh freed the Israelites, and their journey to the Promised Land of Israel began. What did they eat during this time? See Exodus 16:4 and 31.

According to CCC 1094, the manna in the desert prefigured the Eucharist, "the true bread from heaven." Interestingly, the manna was to be collected every single morning. If the Israelites tried to gather extra to save for the next day, they woke up in the morning to find that it stank and was full of worms. This supernatural food was to be gathered as a part of a daily discipline. Throughout the journey to the Promised Land, God was teaching His people how to depend on Him moment by moment, day by day.

3. The eating of the Passover lamb and the manna in the desert both pointed to the Eucharist. You can imagine a New Testament Jew putting it all together, nodding his head and saying, "Yeah . . . I get it! I see the connection!" But there was some Old Testament teaching going on that actually made it harder for New Testament Jews to believe in the Eucharist. In Leviticus 3:17, God forbade the Israelites to consume any blood. Father John Bartunek sheds interesting light on this in the following commentary:

> The Mosaic and Levitical Law prohibited Jews from drinking the blood of their sacrifices, or even eating any meat with the blood still in it. In blood, they believed, was life, and all life belonged to God—it's off-limits for men . . . Pagan religions had no prohibition against the consumption of

blood. Pagans were accustomed to consuming bloody meat and bloody sacrifices. Just as they worshiped idols (creatures that were considered divine), they believed they could enter into communion with the divine through the consumption of those creatures' blood. But the Jews were protected from such practices.[4]

If the Jews were forbidden to consume blood, what might the disciples have thought when Jesus told them to drink His blood?

The only way the Jewish people would have believed that somehow things had changed and it was now OK to drink Jesus' blood would be if they trusted His authority to the same degree that they trusted God the Father's. Jesus ushered in change that could only be received by people who believed He was far more than a prophet, a teacher, or a revolutionary. They needed to believe that He was divine, with authority to bring change to the old way of communing with God.

Quiet your heart and enjoy His presence. . . . Let the Old Testament shed light on the New.

The Passover commemorated the rescue of God's people. The sacrifice of a lamb—its blood on the door, its flesh eaten by the family—brought about that rescue.

The manna in the wilderness was the bread of life to the hungry Israelites, teaching them to depend on God for sustenance every single day.

The Israelites were taught from the very beginning that there was something significant about blood—it contained life, power.

Put it all together:

Jesus, our rescuer, was the final Passover lamb. Today He asks us to consume His body and blood. Jesus invites us to receive the daily spiritual bread of the Eucharist, far more supernatural than manna.

---

[4] Bartunek, *The Better Part: A Christ-Centered Resource for Personal Prayer* (Hamden, CT: Circle Press, 2007), 304.

Jesus invites us to drink His blood in the Eucharist, and in doing so, to share in His divine life. He wants His blood to flow through our veins, giving us the supernatural power to live in freedom.

Spend some time talking to God about what you've studied today. Does it strengthen your faith? Thank Him for that. Do you still have questions? Ask Him. Does it make you long for His presence? He is longing for you, too.

Day Two
HE SAID WHAT HE MEANT

Our reading for today takes place the day after Jesus' miracle of the multiplication of the loaves and fishes. A boy had five barley loaves and two fish, and Jesus multiplied them to feed about five thousand men (plus women and children), with twelve baskets of bread and fish left over. It was a picture of superabundance—another prefiguring of the Eucharist.

Read John 6:22–69 with that miracle in the back of your mind. It's a long reading, I know. But it's just too loaded with good truth to skip bits of it.

As you look at verses 22–34, do you sense the people's hunger? Not just physical hunger, but a yearning for something deeply satisfying? Jesus responds to the hunger with a cryptic comment: "The bread of God is that which comes down from heaven and gives life to the world." And they respond by saying that they want this bread; they are desperate to be filled.

I wonder if Jesus paused at that point. Did He look in their faces, trying to gauge if they were ready for His next words? Were His eyes pleading, hopeful that these people would be able to take the leap of faith that would allow them to embrace what He was going to offer? Jesus saw their emptiness. He knew (and knows!) that only He could satisfy.

1. What did Jesus claim in John 6:35? How did the people react? See John 6:41–42.

2. Instead of backing down because of their critical response to Him, Jesus spoke even more strongly. How did He describe Himself in John 6:48–51? How did the people respond? See John 6:52.

3. Clearly, Jesus' words weren't winning Him any popularity contests. He could have downplayed what He had previously said, or changed the subject. But that's not how He responded. What did He say in verses 53–58?

Some of the deeper meaning of the word *eat* gets lost in translation. Two Greek words, *trogein* and *phagein*, are translated as "eat" in English. At the beginning of the discourse, Jesus used the word *phagein*, which is used to describe a human eating. As He continued speaking, He intensified His word choice and used the word *trogein* instead. *Trogein* is chosen to describe the way an animal eats—more of a gnawing. He had opportunity after opportunity to clarify, correct, or back down. Instead, Jesus' words just got more and more intense.

4. What happened as a result of Jesus' words? See John 6:66.

Many of His followers left and no longer accompanied Him. Make no mistake, Jesus didn't watch with indifference as they walked away. He came to seek and save the lost. His love for each of those retreating souls was so immense that He was soon to die for them. If they had simply misunderstood Him, don't you think He would have chased them down the road to clarify? But if He had meant what He said, simply telling them the truth, the truth He had been waiting throughout the Old Testament to reveal, then He would have had to let them respond as they chose. He never has been one to force Himself on anyone.

Quiet your heart and enjoy His presence. . . . How Jesus longs to satisfy your emptiness.

"Jesus then said to the twelve, 'Do you also want to leave?' Simon Peter answered him, 'Master, to whom shall we go? You have the words of eternal life.'" (John 6:67–68)

So how will we respond? Will we turn away? Or will we take the leap of faith and believe? Will we ask to be filled by the One born in Bethlehem (which means "house of bread")? Will we look for the "food that endures for eternal life" (John 6:27)? The choice is ours. Will we turn away or bow down in worship?

To help bring your heart to a place of worship, listen to Matt Maher's song "Adoration," from his album All the People Said Amen. *It's a contemporary take on the following medieval Latin hymn by Saint Thomas Aquinas.*

"Tantum Ergo"

Down in adoration falling,
This great sacrament we hail
Over ancient forms departing
Newer rites of grace prevail;
Faith for all defects supplying,
Where the feeble senses fail.

To the everlasting Father,
And the Son who reigns on high
With the Spirit blest, proceeding
Forth from each eternally
Be salvation, honor, blessing
Might and endless majesty

Pour upon us, Lord of mercy
Spirit of Thy selfless love
Make of us one true heart yearning
For the glory of thy Son
Jesus, fire of justice blazing
Gladdening light forevermore!

Day Three
JUST KEEPING THE FAITH

I love the way Peter Kreeft describes the Catholic Church. In one of his talks, he compared the Church to a mail carrier: She doesn't write what's delivered or change anything about it; she just delivers it safely. For all that people might not like about the Catholic Church, history proves that she hasn't changed what was originally taught about the Eucharist, regardless of how unpopular or hard to believe it might be. Even Martin Luther didn't deny the real presence of Christ in the Eucharist.[5] This belief went unquestioned for the first thousand years of the Church. That's a pretty long time. In the words of Peter Kreeft:

> The center of all Christian worship until the Reformation was always the Eucharist, not the sermon, as it is for Protestants. The Eucharist was never omitted, as it usually is for Protestants. Any pre-Reformation Christian would see a church service without the Eucharist as something like a marriage without sex. Now comes the supreme irony. What is it that the Eucharist provides? The very thing Protestant Evangelicals cherish the most: the Real Presence of Christ and our real union with Christ, "accepting the Lord Jesus Christ as your personal Savior" in the most real, total, complete, personal, concrete, and intimate way![6]

1. Read CCC 1345 and note the ways in which the Eucharistic celebration has remained consistent throughout the centuries.

2. The earliest written account of the institution of the Lord's Supper in the New Testament is 1 Corinthians 11:23–29. In this passage, Saint Paul describes "handing on what he received from the Lord." What does it mean to eat and drink without "discerning the body"?

---

[5] Luther wrote the following in his *Smalcald Articles*: "Of the Sacrament of the Altar we hold that bread and wine in the Supper are the true body and blood of Christ, and are given and received not only by the godly but also by wicked Christians." He departed from Catholic Church teaching regarding transubstantiation, but never let go of the belief that Christ is present in the Eucharist.

[6] Kreeft, *Jesus Shock*, 107.

3. "From the beginning, the Church has been faithful to the Lord's command" (CCC 1342). Hippolytus of Rome wrote *The Apostolic Tradition* around AD 215. In it, he wrote of the liturgical teachings that had been handed down from the apostles. Here is a section that lays out a script for the ordination of priests:

> PRIEST: The Lord be with you.
> CONGREGATION: And with your spirit.
> PRIEST: Let us lift up our hearts.
> CONGREGATION: We lift them up to the Lord.
> PRIEST: Let us give thanks to the Lord.
> CONGREGATION: It is right and just.[7]

How does reading this impact the way you feel about the celebration of Mass?

Quiet your heart and enjoy His presence. . . . He is unchanging and ever near.

"Behold, I stand at the door and knock; if anyone hears my voice and opens the door, I will come in to him and eat with him, and he with me." (Revelation 3:20)

As we discuss and debate and doubt whether or not He is really present in the Eucharist, Jesus stands at the door of our hearts and knocks. He wants to intimately enter the deepest part of who we are to give us His divine life. Many of us don't open the door because we don't realize who is on the other side. He's been faithfully doing this for centuries, never giving up, because His love for us is never failing. Whether we recognize Him in this hidden form doesn't change reality. He is there. He waits.

He longs for true intimacy with you—for a connection that is soul deep and personal. Open the door of your heart and never be lonely again.

---

7 Scott Hahn, *The Lamb's Supper: The Mass as Heaven on Earth* (New York: Random House, 1999), 37–38.

Day Four
THE KEY TO SAINTHOOD: A FIRE HOSE OF GRACE

Before I could even look at the benefits of the Eucharist, I had to understand where it came from. Just being told to believe wasn't enough. A wonderful priest was kind enough to teach me the very things we've explored in Days One to Three. Once I understood that this wasn't some new teaching, that if I interpreted John 6 literally this was the only possible conclusion, and recognized that for a thousand years this was the unchallenged teaching of the Church, my heart settled and got incredibly excited. There was *more* for me to discover about Christ. I could get closer to Jesus than I previously had.

Do you want to become a saint? I'm not talking about wanting recognition for your holiness. A saint is simply someone who has been radically transformed by Christ. She has pursued Jesus wholeheartedly, and in that pursuit has been changed for the better.

This is what I long for and one of the reasons I find it such a privilege to be Catholic. Two of the most effective ways to become a saint are through Eucharistic adoration and receiving Christ in the Eucharist. This isn't because doing these things checks a box or makes us poster-child Catholics. It's because Jesus is a saint maker. And wherever He is, He is at work. His presence burns away the things that don't resemble Him, and fans into flame the love that allows us to live as He did.

1. What is the principal fruit of receiving the Eucharist? See CCC 1391.

The principal fruit of the Eucharist isn't some*thing* Jesus gives us; it's some*one*. It's the gift of *Himself.* All too often, we are overwhelmed by our problems and underwhelmed by our humble Savior, who waits to be invited in. Yet He is the answer to all our deepest longings and the fulfillment of our greatest needs.

2. What is strengthened and what is wiped away when we receive the Eucharist? See CCC 1394.

3. You may wonder if everyone who receives the Eucharist has the same experience. The answer is no. Peter Kreeft (yet again) nails it with this explanation: "Sacraments are like hoses. They are the channels of the living water of God's grace. Our faith is like opening the faucet. We can open it a lot, a little, or not at all. When the faucet handle is turned off, no water flows to us, even though the water is still objectively present. When it is 'turned on' by faith, the water flows out and into us and we get wet."[8]

No, not everyone has the same experience at Communion, but it's up to us how open we want to be. If you are Catholic, how do you typically receive the sacrament of the Eucharist? Do you open the faucet a lot or a little? What do you think might help you to turn the faucet on full blast?

Quiet your heart and enjoy His presence. . . . His fire hose of grace is pointed at your heart at every Mass.

Jesus,

You are the bread of life. You are what I am hungering for. I may run after all sorts of things that will never satisfy me, yet you never give up on me. What other response can I give you than to draw as close to you as humanly possible, and then bow before you? Oh God, shower me with your grace! Not just a trickle, but a waterfall! Cleanse me; change me; make me more like you.

Forgive me for all the times I've received you with indifference or disbelief. Thank you for your patience with me. Light a fire within me that only intensifies over time. Save me from living numb or short of all you have prepared for me. You promise an abundant life, a feast prepared in the presence of my enemies (Psalm 23:5). May I never content myself with junk food again. Satisfy my deepest yearnings with your real presence!

---

[8] Kreeft, *Jesus Shock*, 117.

Day Five
SAINT'S STORY

Saint Clare

In the mid-thirteenth century, Saracen mercenaries were storming the city of Assisi, in Italy. They had entered the monastery of San Damiano, intending to raid and loot the convent, and had penetrated the inner cloister, where the sisters trembled and cried out in fear.

Clare, daughter of a wealthy Italian family, who was inspired to give her life in service to Christ when she heard the teachings of Francis of Assisi, knew she had to act to try to save her sisters. She rose and went to the chapel. She took the silver and gold monstrance to the window overlooking the enemy. The soldiers were a dark mass of movement down below; their weapons gleamed in the moonlight and their crude shouts echoed in the courtyard. She placed the monstrance with the Host on the windowsill in sight of the men, and she prostrated herself in prayer like Queen Esther before her king. In tears, she begged, "Behold, my Lord, is it possible that you want to deliver your defenseless handmaids, whom I have taught out of love for you, into the hands of pagans?" She begged Him to protect them, since she was powerless to protect them herself. Then, a voice like that of a child echoed in her ears: "I will always protect you!"

Clare also prayed for the city, and the voice answered, "It will have to undergo trials, but it will be defended by My protection." At these words, she lifted her face from the stones and told the sisters, "I assure you, daughters, that you will suffer no evil. Only have faith in Christ." Shortly after, the Saracens took flight, scaling the walls in their haste to depart.

Jesus had spoken, and He had acted from the Eucharist, where He is truly present. It is not only in the past that He has acted. It is today, now, with you. Do you believe that all of your enemies—the problems that plague you, the stresses that take away your peace of heart, the sins you cannot seem to conquer, the sins of others that weigh on your heart and bring suffering into your home—can be vanquished from your place of prayer before the Eucharist?

The sacrament on the altar is not a thing; it is a person. It is He, Jesus, who waits for us there. It is He, alive. He listens, He understands, He speaks. And when we are distant, He gently calls our name. He brings us home again. Jesus in the Eucharist is always at work in a gentle, powerful, but often hidden way. But there are times when

He allows us to see His hand so that we can praise Him and "remember the works of the Lord" (Psalm 77:11).

Prayer, do not forget, is a conversation with your best friend, with the One who will never, ever abandon you. How much more powerful, then, is your conversation with this friend *in the flesh*, in the Blessed Sacrament, where He is really present! It is there that His eyes look upon you with so much love, His hands reach out to console you, His words penetrate your heart like a river of peace, and His soul embraces you and draws you into Him. You may not see it; you may not feel it; but He is there, and He is acting in your life.

Jesus said, "A man can have no greater love than to lay down his life for a friend" (John 15:13). He laid Himself down for Clare and the sisters that day when the Saracens were invading. Like a good shepherd, He placed His body between them and the enemy. But He also lays Himself down for you every day in every tabernacle in the world. He waits for you there, the great friend who understands all of your problems, who accepts you as you are, and who wants to heal and save you.

This great friend has come from heaven to be with you. Will you not go to Him?

What does Saint Clare's story reveal to you about the role the Eucharist plays in our friendship with Jesus?

Conclusion

Jesus has made a way for all of us to enter into a life-changing relationship with Him, but He is a gentleman; He waits to be invited in. Will you do that now? Will you invite Him to intersect your life with power and authority? Are you ready to stop trying to control it all yourself? Are you ready for freedom?

Do you long for more?

Oh, friends. There is more. It's just that we've settled for less than what God is holding out to us. Aren't you ready to let the religiosity, pride, cynicism, and hopelessness go, and instead step out in faith?

Ask the Lord for eyes to see. Is the Eucharist any more unbelievable than the Incarnation? Both are mind-boggling. Both require recognizing God in a hidden form—one is a wafer; the other is a human body. To wrap your mind around either of those miracles is a pretty tall order. That's why we need faith. Faith is believing without seeing (2 Corinthians 5:7). And the beautiful thing is that we don't need to conjure up faith when we lack it. We can ask God to give it to us. Ask God to give you the gift of faith, and then follow the example of Saint Augustine, who said, "I believe so that I may understand."

Jesus will always refuse to fit into a box. He won't conform to our definitions. He won't be controlled. He won't be molded into some version of a deity that pleases us. He approaches us as He chooses, and as wild as it may seem to us, the Eucharist is how He has chosen to draw near. He is beyond our ability to comprehend. "The foolishness of God is wiser than human wisdom, and the weakness of God is stronger than human strength" (1 Corinthians 1:25). Our minds can't wrap around or contain Him.

One last thing: When you receive Christ in the Eucharist, lack of feelings is *not* proof that nothing is happening. It's a reminder that God doesn't want us to be "experience junkies," relying on our emotions. What is it that pleases Him most of all? Faith.

~A faith that says, "Regardless of what I've done, I know that Jesus' sacrifice purchased forgiveness for me and it is enough."

~A faith that says, "As crazy as it seems, the God of the universe has made Himself small and *wants me*."

~A faith that says, "I'm not worshipping a dead Savior. He is alive. And active. And even though I can't see Him, I know that wherever He is, He is at work."

He's issued you the invitation. Will you draw near?

My Resolution

In what specific way will I apply what I have learned in this lesson?

Examples:

1. *I want more of Jesus!* Because of this, I'm going to go to Mass more frequently this week. I'll go on _____ in addition to Sunday.

2. I will spend time with the Lord in adoration on _____, asking Him to shower me with His love and grace.

3. Before I receive the Eucharist, I'll spend some time in prayer telling God that I am turning the faucet *all the way on* because I want everything He has for me.

My resolution:

Catechism Clips

CCC 1094 It is on this harmony of the two Testaments that the Paschal catechesis of the Lord is built, and then, that of the Apostles and the Fathers of the Church. This catechesis unveils what lay hidden under the letter of the Old Testament: the mystery of Christ. It is called "typological" because it reveals the newness of Christ on the basis of the "figures" (types) which announce him in the deeds, words, and symbols of the first covenant. By this re-reading in the Spirit of Truth, starting from Christ, the figures are unveiled. Thus the flood and Noah's ark prefigured salvation by Baptism, as did the cloud and the crossing of the Red Sea. Water from the rock was the figure of the Spiritual gifts of Christ, and manna in the desert prefigured the Eucharist, "the true bread from heaven."

CCC 1345 As early as the second century we have the witness of St. Justin Martyr for the basic lines of the order of the Eucharistic celebration. They have stayed the same until our own day for all the great liturgical families. St. Justin wrote to the pagan emperor Antonius Pius (138–161) around the year 155, explaining what Christians did:

On the day we call the day of the sun, all who dwell in the city or country gather in the same place.

The memoirs of the apostles and the writings of the prophets are read, as much as time permits.

When the reader has finished, he who presides over those gathered admonishes and challenges them to imitate these beautiful things.

Then we all rise together and offer prayers for ourselves . . . and for all others, wherever they may be, so that we may be found righteous by our life and actions, and faithful to the commandments, so as to obtain eternal salvation.

When the prayers are concluded we exchange the kiss.

Then someone brings bread and a cup of water and wine mixed together to him who presides over the brethren.

He takes them and offers praise and glory to the Father of the universe, through the name of the Son and of the Holy Spirit and for a considerable time he gives thanks (in Greek: *eucharistian*) that we have been judged worthy of these gifts.

When he has concluded the prayers and thanksgivings, all present give voice to an acclamation by saying: "Amen."

When he who presides has given thanks and the people have responded, those whom we call deacons give to those present the "eucharisted" bread, wine and water and take them to those who are absent.

CCC 1391 Holy Communion augments our union with Christ. The principal fruit of receiving the Eucharist in Holy Communion is an intimate union with Christ Jesus. Indeed, the Lord said: "He who eats my flesh and drinks my blood abides in me, and I in him." Life in Christ has its foundation in the Eucharistic banquet: "As the living Father sent me, and I live because of the Father, so he who eats me will live because of me."

On the feasts of the Lord, when the faithful receive the Body of the Son, they proclaim to one another the Good News that the first fruits of life have been given, as when the angel said to Mary Magdalene, "Christ is risen!" Now too are life and resurrection conferred on whoever receives Christ.

CCC 1394 As bodily nourishment restores lost strength, so the Eucharist strengthens our charity, which tends to be weakened in daily life; and this living charity wipes away venial sins. By giving himself to us Christ revives our love and enables us to break our disordered attachments to creatures and root ourselves in him:

Since Christ died for us out of love, when we celebrate the memorial of his death at the moment of sacrifice we ask that love may be granted to us by the coming of the Holy Spirit. We humbly pray that in the strength of this love by which Christ willed to die for us, we, by receiving the gift of the Holy Spirit, may be able to consider the world as crucified for us, and to be ourselves as crucified to the world. Having received the gift of love, let us die to sin and live for God.

Lesson 3

EMBRACED BY MERCY ~ WE NEED RECONCILIATION

Introduction

No doubt about it, our view of God will affect how we feel about the sacrament of reconciliation. Some of us think of God as a stern father or an authoritarian dictator. We might picture Him with a face of constant disapproval. We think to ourselves, "Why go to confession and spend time in front of someone who is never going to approve of me, anyway? Why bother? I'll never be good enough."

Some of us think of God as an indulgent father, one who wants us to be happy, and who laughs at our foolish mistakes, never really taking things too seriously. He is our cosmic good buddy—our cheerleader. This image of God, although it contains some truth, is incomplete, and it can cause us not to go to confession because we simply don't take our sins very seriously.

Our feelings about the sacrament of penance aren't impacted just by our view of God. We're also influenced by our culture's sensitivity (or lack thereof) to sin. According to Peter Kreeft, "We usually think we are morally pretty good because we measure ourselves, not against the standards of our Lord, but against the standards of society."[9] And our society excuses quite a lot.

This means we tend to waver between feeling like the sacrament of penance is totally unnecessary because we are basically good people and feeling like it may be necessary, but it's the last place we want to go. Either way, the confessional lines stay pretty short on Saturday afternoons.

---

[9] Peter J. Kreeft, *Catholic Christianity: A Complete Catechism of Catholic Church Beliefs Based on the Catechism of the Catholic Church* (San Francisco: Ignatius Press, 2001).

The purpose of this lesson is to look at what the sacrament of penance has to do with our friendship with Christ. Make no mistake—**this sacrament is not about condemnation. Its purpose is to heal and reconcile our relationship with our truest, most faithful friend.** This may not be the way it was presented to you in the past. If that's the case, you may have to let go of some preconceived notions of how God sees and relates to you. I know this isn't easy to do. It's hard to give things a second chance when they've caused us pain.

Many of us have negative memories of confessing our sins to a priest. For those of us who are feeling a little uneasy about this lesson, perhaps the following words from theologian Jean Vanier will offer comfort: "Somewhere along the line in the history of the Church, people have become more centered upon obedience to laws than upon this relationship of love with a person, with Jesus; more centered upon justice than upon love. The heart of our faith is not law, it is a person, Jesus who calls us into the peace and joy of friendship and of love."[10]

My prayer this week is that we will look at the sacrament with fresh eyes and an ever-increasing awareness of God's desire to blanket us with mercy. He doesn't approach His children with the law in one hand and a scowl on His face. He's the father of the Prodigal Son, and He runs toward us with open arms. He never gives up on us. Can you personalize that truth? He hasn't given up on *you*.

Day One
OUR TRUEST FRIEND'S PROMISE

Read the first two pages of Appendix 3, "Confession by the Numbers."

1. What are the 9 Confession Promises described in this article?

---

[10] Father Paul Farren, *Freedom and Forgiveness: A Fresh Look at the Sacrament of Reconciliation* (Dublin: Columba Press, 2013), x.

2. Which of the 9 Confession Promises do you need the most?

3. One of the 9 Confession Promises is a new heart. In the sacrament of penance, we offer God our callused and hardened hearts. In exchange, He gives us hearts that are tender and more sensitive to sin's damaging effects. CCC 1432 says, "God must give man a new heart. . . . It is in discovering the greatness of God's love that our heart is shaken by the horror and weight of our sin," which strengthens us so we can make better choices in the future.

Look up the following verses that speak of the greatness of God's love, then put them in your own words. These are great verses to read and think about before receiving the sacrament of penance because they keep our focus on His steadfast promise of mercy.

Exodus 34:6

Isaiah 49:15

Ephesians 2:4–5

Quiet your heart and enjoy His presence. . . . He offers pardon and peace.

"Let us hold unwaveringly to our confession that gives us hope, for he who made the promise is trustworthy." (Hebrews 10:23)

This is truth we can count on. The One who made the promises we've read about today is trustworthy. He always comes through. He is consistently faithful to His word.

What word does He speak over our mistakes and regrets and failures? Mercy.

Mercy trumps justice. Every time. Justice looks at what is deserved. It demands punishment for all the times we have failed to love others as we should. But God's mercy proves stronger than what is "fair."

No matter how numerous your shortcomings, don't lose hope. God took every one of them into account before you were even born, and made sure that His steadfast mercy would be enough to cover them all.

These are His words for you today:

"Do not be afraid, I have redeemed you. I have called you by name; you are mine. You are precious in my eyes. You are honored and I love you. Do not be afraid. I am with you." (Isaiah 43:1, 4)

Day Two
OUR TRUEST FRIEND KNOWS WHAT'S BEST FOR US

Read the second page of Appendix 3, "Confession by the Numbers." This section is titled "10 Reasons to Confess."

1. According to this section, what are five *human* reasons to go to confession? Note: A "human reason" is something that directs us toward growing into more mature and virtuous humans. It makes us more pleasant to be around. This is different from a spiritual reason, which goes deeper on a soul level.

   A.

   B.

   C.

   D.

   E.

2. Which of the five human reasons resonates most with you?

3. According to the article, what are five *spiritual* reasons to go to confession?

   A.

   B.

   C.

   D.

   E.

4. Which of the five spiritual reasons resonates most with you?

Quiet your heart and enjoy His presence. . . . He knows us better than we know ourselves.

Our self-perception can get pretty messed up. There are times we go too easy on ourselves, excusing things that God takes seriously. Under other circumstances, we can go to the opposite extreme and hopelessly condemn ourselves. This is why there is enormous benefit in unpacking our sins alongside a priest who can guide us objectively.

In his book Interior Freedom, *Father Jacques Philippe writes about how important it is for us to have a realistic view of ourselves:*

> *One of the most essential conditions for God's grace to act in our lives is saying yes to what we are and to the situations in which we find ourselves. That is because God is "realistic." His grace does not operate on our imaginings, ideals, or dreams. It works on reality . . . The*

person God loves with the tenderness of a Father, the person he wants to touch and to transform with his love, is not the person we'd have liked to be or ought to be. It's the person we are. God doesn't love "ideal persons" or "virtual beings." He loves actual, real people.[11]

What we need in confession is an honest, truthful assessment that brings us back to an awareness of who we are and whose we are. We are beloved, and we belong. This message is at the heart of the sacrament of penance. This is the grace God is whispering to our souls.

Father Paul Farren has this to say about God's message to us in the confessional: "When we think about the sacrament of Reconciliation our thoughts most often focus on ourselves and our sinfulness. The role of God in some sense might even appear secondary. However, the sacrament of Reconciliation is primarily that sacred place and moment when God confesses. . . . What does God confess? God confesses his love, his forgiveness, his gratitude, his confidence, his trust and his belief in us."[12]

Spend some time in prayer thanking God for His love, His forgiveness, His gratitude, His confidence, His trust, and His belief in you.

Day Three
OUR TRUEST FRIEND WANTS AN INTIMATE RELATIONSHIP WITH US

1. According to CCC 1468, what is the "whole power" of the sacrament of penance based on?

2. We read in Genesis that in the beginning, God *walked around* in the Garden of Eden. His relationship with Adam and Eve was intimate, authentic, and face-to-face. There was no sin. There was no shame. There was nothing to separate them. What impact did Adam and Eve's sin have on their relationship with God? See Genesis 3:8–10.

---

[11] Philippe, *Interior Freedom*, 32.
[12] Farren, *Freedom and Forgiveness*, 1.

God has never stopped longing for a renewal of that authentic, intimate friendship. This is why He sent Jesus to earth—to provide a means for us to approach Him with the confidence of a child who knows she belongs to her father.

But all too often, what we experience is distance in that relationship. This is not because God has moved away from us. We are the ones who turn away. We do this in all sorts of ways: We hide in fear, hang our heads in shame, or stick up our noses in pride. We'll do anything to avoid making eye contact with God.

It reminds me of times my kids have done something wrong and I'm trying to discipline them. Sometimes they respond with their arms folded, staring at the floor in anger. They are mad that they've been caught. Other times their faces are in their hands, and they can't stop crying because they are so upset for messing up. No matter what the heart attitude, what I really want them to do is look me in the eye. I want this for two reasons. One is for them to know that I'm serious about what I'm saying. But I also want them to see the unconditional love in my eyes.

When God invites us to the sacrament of penance, He's asking us to look Him in the eye. He wants to make eye contact with us. In that moment, we can see ourselves from His perspective. Yes, our sin is serious. He isn't saying that it doesn't matter. But it doesn't diminish His love for us. In the confessional, we look the Lord in the eye and experience a moment of deep tenderness as God whispers, "It's OK. Come out of hiding. You're safe here with me."

3. Is there anything that is holding you back from the sacrament of penance?

Quiet your heart and enjoy His presence. . . . "May the eyes of your heart be enlightened, that you may know what is the hope that belongs to his call" (Ephesians 1:18).

Friend, the Lord is calling you. He is inviting you to come and gaze into His eyes of mercy. He's offering you hope for a fresh start. Oh, I pray that the eyes of your heart would be enlightened, and that the darkness of shame would be chased away. Shame keeps your eyes cast down. But God is cupping your face in His hands and calling you to look up.

Dear Lord,

I get so nervous at the thought of looking in your eyes. I don't know if I'm ready to see myself reflected in them. I feel shame over things I've said and done, and I wonder how you could possibly forgive me.

But then I look at the cross, and am reminded that while I was still a sinner, you died for me (Romans 5:8). Your love for me isn't dependent on what I do. It depends on what you have done for me. So give me the confidence to approach your throne of grace. I know I am promised that what I will encounter there is mercy. Always. Without exception.

"Who will bring a charge against God's chosen ones? It is God who acquits us. Who will condemn? It is Christ who died, rather, was raised, who also is at the right hand of God, who indeed intercedes for us. What will separate us from the love of Christ? Will anguish, or distress, or persecution, or famine, or nakedness, or peril, or the swords? . . . No, in all these things we conquer overwhelmingly through him who loved us. For I am convinced that neither death, nor life, nor angels, nor principalities, nor present things, nor future things, nor powers, nor height, nor depth, nor any other creature will be able to separate us from the love of God in Christ Jesus our Lord." (Romans 8:33–35, 37–39)

Day Four
OUR TRUEST FRIEND WANTS US TO LIVE IN FREEDOM

1. In John 8:36, we are promised, "If the son sets you free, you will be free indeed." Yet so many Christians don't feel they are experiencing spiritual freedom. One of the reasons for this is described in John 8:34. According to that verse, what gets in the way of our freedom?

Saint Paul addresses this in Galatians 5:1 with the words, "For freedom Christ set us free; so stand firm and do not submit again to the yoke of slavery." All too often, we take our freedom and use it to step right back into the bondage of slavery to sin. We get into bad habits that we don't feel able to break. We harbor bitterness and it keeps our hearts in a vise grip. Our words seem to take on a life of their own and are out of our mouths before we can stop them. We feel dominated by sin, and aren't sure how to get free.

This is where the sacrament of penance comes in. We don't go to the confessional just for forgiveness. There is more.

2. How is the "more" of the sacrament of penance described in the last part of CCC 1496?

Friends, this is it. This is the secret to growing stronger spiritually. When we receive absolution in the sacrament of penance, we receive supernatural grace to help us go back out into our lives strengthened and fortified in the very areas where we feel the weakest. We get a second wind and find that we are able to keep pursuing the summit. Theologian Scott Hahn describes it this way:

> Through confession, we begin to heal. We begin to get our story straight and stop deceiving ourselves. We come home to resume our place in the family of God. We begin to know peace. None of this comes easily. Confession doesn't make change easy, but it does make it possible. It is not a quick fix, but it is a sure cure. We need to go back to the sacrament, and go again, and keep going back, because life is a marathon, not a forty-yard dash. We'll often want to stop, but like a distance runner, we'll need to press on for our second wind, and third, and fourth. In this case, we can count on the wind coming, because it's the "wind" of the Holy Spirit.[13]

3. The "wind" of the Holy Spirit is exactly what we need to persevere in the Christian life. According to 2 Corinthians 3:17, what else does the presence of the Holy Spirit bring us?

Quiet your heart and enjoy His presence. . . . The truth will set you free.

Our truest friend knows how much we need freedom. Father Jacques Philippe writes, "Our freedom is proportionate to the love and childlike trust we have for our heavenly Father."[14] The more we

---

[13] Scott Hahn, *Lord, Have Mercy: The Healing Power of Confession* (New York: Doubleday, 2003), 175.
[14] Philippe, *Interior Freedom* (New York: Scepter Publishers, 2002), 15.

meditate on His character—His mercy, His love, and His forgiving nature—the more our trust in Him will grow.

He is waiting for you. He is longing to fill you with the peace and freedom that come from hearing that you are beloved. That you belong. That you are forgiven.

"He is lover. He is redeemer. He is father. He is friend. He is our shelter. He is our healer. He is the lifter of our heads."[15] —Meredith Andrews

"The look in his eyes is the purest, truest, tenderest, most loving, and most hope-filled in this world."[16] —Father Jacques Philippe

Day Five
SAINT'S STORY

Saint Faustina Reveals God's Mercy

God never gives up on us. This is what we mean when we say that God is merciful. Instead of giving the human race what its sins deserved, He sent His Son to redeem us.

"[H]e predestined us to be adopted as His sons through Jesus Christ, in accordance with His pleasure and will—to the praise of His glorious grace, which He has freely given us in the One He loves. In [Christ] we have redemption through His blood, the forgiveness of sins, in accordance with the riches of God's grace that He lavished on us with all wisdom and understanding." (Ephesians 1:5–8)

Yet, He will not force us to accept the priceless gift of His grace and forgiveness: "O Jerusalem, Jerusalem, you who kill the prophets and stone those sent to you, how often I have longed to gather your children together, as a hen gathers her chicks under her wings, but you were not willing!" (Luke 13:34)

The sacrament of confession proves this: God is always ready to forgive, but He respects our freedom too much to do so unless we really want Him to, and unless we repent. And so He gives us the perfect opportunity to show that we really want His

---

[15] Meredith Andrews, "Lift Up Your Head," *The Invitation* (Nashville, TN: Word Entertainment, 2008), compact disc.
[16] Philippe, *Interior Freedom*, 36.

forgiveness: the sacrament of reconciliation. Confession is the "tribunal of mercy," as Jesus Himself described it to Saint Faustina Kowalska.

Saint Faustina died in 1938 in her convent in Krakow, Poland, when she was only thirty-three, her body torn asunder by tuberculosis and a host of other illnesses and suffering. At the time, few guessed what an extraordinary saint she was. But when her diary, *Divine Mercy in My Soul*, was published, word spread fast, and she was recognized as Christ's specially chosen apostle of the Divine Mercy.

She had entered the convent when she was twenty, after an uneventful but pious childhood. For the next thirteen years she would live in four different convents of the same religious congregation, the Sisters of Our Lady of Mercy, and serve as cook, gardener, and doorkeeper—hardly a glamorous résumé. But in those years her intimate union with Christ deepened steadily under the subtle action of grace, and she was granted visions, revelations, hidden stigmata, participation in the Lord's Passion, bilocation, the ability to read souls, the gift of prophecy, and the privilege of mystical engagement and marriage.

All these gifts were directed toward helping Saint Faustina fulfill her threefold mission of reminding the world of God's powerful, loving mercy, sparking a new devotion to that mercy, and founding the Apostolic Movement of the Divine Mercy. All three were successfully carried out in her brief but intense life.

In her famous diary, she recorded many things that our Lord spoke to her. One of His favorite topics was the sacrament of reconciliation. From His comments, it is clear that He has a special love for that sacrament as a unique and powerful place of encounter between a soul who recognizes its need for grace, and Himself, who is so eager to meet that need. Here are some of our Lord's words to Saint Faustina:

> [Today the Lord said to me,] Daughter, when you go to confession, to this fountain of My mercy, the Blood and Water which came forth from My Heart always flows down upon your soul and ennobles it. Every time you go to confession, immerse yourself entirely in My mercy, with great trust, so that I may pour the bounty of My grace upon your soul. When you approach the confessional, know this: that I Myself am waiting there for you. I am only hidden by the priest, but I Myself act in your soul. Here the misery of the soul meets the God of mercy.[17] (Diary entry 1602)

---

[17] Saint Maria Faustina Kowalska, *Diary of Saint Maria Faustina Kowalska: Divine Mercy in My Soul* (Stockbridge, MA: Marian Press, 2005), 352–53.

Write, speak of My mercy. Tell souls where they are to look for solace; that is, in the Tribunal of Mercy [the sacrament of reconciliation]. There the greatest miracles take place [and] are incessantly repeated. To avail oneself of this miracle, it is not necessary to go on a great pilgrimage or to carry out some external ceremony; it suffices to come with faith to the feet of My representative and to reveal to him one's misery, and the miracle of Divine Mercy will be fully demonstrated. Were a soul like a decaying corpse so that from a human standpoint, there would be no [hope of] restoration and everything would already be lost, it is not so with God. The miracle of Divine Mercy restores that soul in full. Oh, how miserable are those who do not take advantage of the miracle of God's mercy! You will call out in vain, but it will be too late.[18] (Diary entry 1448)

How does Saint Faustina's description of God's mercy affect your feelings toward the sacrament of penance?

What can you take away from her life that might strengthen your faith?

Conclusion

There is a song I haven't been able to get out of my head as I've written this lesson. It's my current favorite, and because of the truth of the words, I think I'm going to love this song forever. To me, it summarizes perfectly what God is inviting us to through the sacrament of penance. I leave you with its lyrics, and am praying that you'll be able to listen to the actual song and to close your eyes as you play it. If I were with you, I'd have you sit down and would put headphones on your ears. It doesn't matter how many times I hear it; it gets me every time. We are so crazy loved by our God. If we could just grasp how much, we would be utterly changed.

May God call to your heart through these words.

"Out of Hiding" (from the album *The Undoing*, by Steffany Gretzinger)

Come out of hiding, you're safe here with me
There's no need to cover what I already see
You've got your reasons but I hold your peace
You've been on lockdown and I hold the key

---

[18] Ibid., 319.

'Cause I loved you before you knew it was love
And I saw it all, still I chose the cross
And you were the one that I was thinking of when I rose from the grave
Now rid of the shackles my victory's yours
I tore the veil so you could come close
There's no reason to stand at a distance anymore
You're not far from home

I'll be your lighthouse when you're lost at sea
And I will illuminate everything
No need to be frightened of intimacy
No, just throw off your fear and come running to me
And oh, as you run, what hindered love will only become part of the story
You're almost home now . . . please don't quit now . . . you're almost home to me.[19]

My Resolution

In what specific way will I apply what I have learned in this lesson?

Examples:

1. It's been a while since I've received the sacrament of penance and I'm nervous that I won't know what to do. I'll prepare by reading the section of Appendix 3 titled "7 Things Expected from You in Confession."

2. I'll receive the sacrament of penance this week, using the sections of Appendix 3 titled "6 Ways to Examine Your Conscience" and "10 Commandments" to help me prepare.

3. If shame and fear are keeping me from receiving all the promises and benefits of the sacrament of penance, I will take time each day this week to meditate on God's unchanging love for me. I'll do this by meditating on Romans 8:33–39.

---

[19] Steffany Gretzinger, "Out of Hiding," *The Undoing* (Redding, CA: Bethel Music, 2014), compact disc.

My resolution:

Catechism Clips

CCC 1468 "The whole power of the sacrament of Penance consists in restoring us to God's grace and joining us with him in an intimate friendship." Reconciliation with God is thus the purpose and effect of this sacrament. For those who receive the sacrament of Penance with contrite heart and religious disposition, reconciliation "is usually followed by peace and serenity of conscience with strong spiritual consolation." Indeed the sacrament of Reconciliation with God brings about a true "spiritual resurrection," restoration of the dignity and blessings of the life of the children of God, of which the most precious is friendship with God.

CCC 1496 The spiritual effects of the sacrament of Penance are:

-Reconciliation with God by which the penitent recovers grace;
-Reconciliation with the Church;
-Remission of the eternal punishment incurred by mortal sins;
-Remission, at least in part, of temporal punishments resulting from sin;
-Peace and serenity of conscience, and spiritual consolation;
-An increase of spiritual strength for the Christian battle.

Lesson 4

OUR REFUGE ~ WE NEED A MOTHER

Introduction

Technology today has made it possible to communicate with people at an unprecedented rate. 15,220,700 texts are sent every minute of every day worldwide.[20] Social media sites such as Twitter and Facebook give us even more opportunities to connect, with users sending 6000 tweets per second (think 500 million tweets per day)[21] and the connection of 2 billion worldwide Facebook users.[22]   It makes me picture millions of hearts yearning to be known, to be understood—to be seen. Although stats like these make it clear that we are reaching out, current research also shows that 25 percent of Americans say they don't have anyone they can talk to about their personal troubles.[23]

The truth is, we are growing increasingly socially isolated while online social networks are exploding. We are seeking connection, but so many of our connections aren't satisfying. Too many of our relationships feel superficial, artificial, one step removed from the real thing. This isolation can be soul deadening.

We long for a soft place to land, a place characterized by unconditional love made more powerful and healing through gentle truth telling.

We are craving a family.

In John 14:18, Jesus promised, "I will not leave you as orphans." God has given us a spiritual family—a heavenly Father, a heavenly mother, and the best older brother

---

[20] "73 Texting Statistics that Answer All Your Questions", textrequest.com, https://www.textrequest.com/blog/texting-statistics-answer-questions/, accessed September 29, 2017.

[21] "Twitter Usage Statistics," internetlivestats.com, http://www.internetlivestats.com/twitter-statistics/, accessed September 29, 2017.

[22] "Facebook now has 2 Billion Monthly Users and…Responsibility," techcrunch.com, https://techcrunch.com/2017/06/27/facebook-2-billion-users/, accessed Septembe 29, 2017.

[23] Johannah Cornblatt, "Lonely Planet: Isolation Increases in the US," *Newsweek*, August 20, 2009, http://www.newsweek.com/lonely-planet-isolation-increases-us-78647.

imaginable. We are children of God, adopted into a family. We belong. This is where we are cherished and protected. We discover a safe haven in the context of these relationships.

The Catholic Church has always believed that when Jesus hung on the cross in John 19, His final words to the apostle John and His mother, Mary, had meaning for the entire Church. When Jesus said to Mary, "Woman, behold, your son," and to John, "Behold your mother," Mary was being given the role of mother of all Christians. "Mary had only one Son, Jesus, but in Him, her spiritual motherhood extends to all whom He came to save" (*Compendium of the Catechism of the Catholic Church* 100).

In his book *Hail, Holy Queen*, Scott Hahn writes, "Every family needs a mother; only Christ could choose His own, and He chose providentially for His entire covenant family . . . For a family is incomplete without a loving mother. The breakaway Christian churches that diminish Mary's role inevitably end up feeling like a bachelor's apartment: masculine to a fault; orderly but not homey; functional and productive—but with little sense of beauty and poetry."[24]

Mary invites us home and longs to mother each of her children in a very personal way. Father Michael Gaitley unpacks this truth in his book *33 Days to Morning Glory: A Do-It-Yourself Retreat in Preparation for Marian Consecration*:

> Mary's new motherhood is not some vague or abstract sort of thing. It's concrete and personal. And even though it's universal, it's also intensely particular. Mary is your mother. She is my mother. In this light, Saint John Paul II thinks it's significant that Mary's new motherhood on Calvary is expressed in the singular, "Behold, your son" not "Behold, your billions of spiritual children." The Pope gets to the heart of it when he says, "Even when the same woman is the mother of many children, her personal relationship with each one of them is of the very essence of motherhood." In short: Mary is uniquely, particularly, personally your mother and my mother, and she doesn't lose us in the crowd.[25]

What does Mary have to do with our relationship with Christ? As our heavenly mother, she wants what is best for us. She knows that so many of our attempts to connect and be known by people around us will fill the hours, but never the heart. Because of this, she never stops pointing us toward the only One who will truly satisfy our inner longing for belonging, safety, and love. She always leads us home to her Son.

---

[24] Scott Hahn, *Hail, Holy Queen: The Mother of God in the Word of God* (New York: Doubleday) 27–28.
[25] Michael E. Gaitley, *33 Days to Morning Glory: A Do-It-Yourself Retreat in Preparation for Marian Consecration* (Stockbridge, MA: Marian Press, 2011), 99.

Day One
MARY: FULL OF GRACE

We don't just want to have a friendship with Christ; we want to grow more and more like Him. We want to be changed. In our efforts to follow Christ and more closely resemble Him, no greater example exists than the Blessed Mother. From the first moment we meet her in Scripture, she stands out as the supreme model of a woman so full of God that there's no room for selfishness, fear, or bitterness. There's only grace.

Read Luke 1:26–38.

1. A. What does the angel Gabriel call Mary in Luke 1:28?

The word translated "favored one" is *kecharitōmenē* in the original Greek language, and means "to endow with grace" or to be "full of grace." In his book *Walking with Mary*, Dr. Edward Sri observes, "In Luke 1:28, [kecharitōmenē] appears in the passive tense, which underscores how Mary's special favor is based on God's activity in her life. Mary is the recipient of this unique grace."[26] It's God's gift to her.

B. Some of us are motivated by Mary's holiness, and others feel that emulating her is impossible because she's just too good. It's interesting that the root word used in Luke 1:28 is also used in Ephesians 1:5–8. Read that passage and note what is lavished on God's children—on *us*.

---

[26] Edward Sri, *Walking with Mary: A Biblical Journey from Nazareth to the Cross* (New York: Crown Publishing Group, 2013), 42.

Yes, God filled Mary with divine grace from the very beginning—from her conception. True, she didn't start life with original sin the way we do. Nevertheless, God has given us everything we need today to make the right choices, to reflect Mary's character in all we do and say.

2. The angel Gabriel knew that the shock of his arrival and the news he was about to give Mary was terrifying. What words did he use to comfort her? See Luke 1:28 and 30.

3. What was Mary's response to the angel's shocking revelation? See Luke 1:38.

4. We will all encounter times when God intersects our plans with one of His own. Just like Mary, we'll have to choose between following God and insisting on our own way. More often than not, His plan will seem cloaked in shadows—we won't clearly see exactly how it's all going to roll out. In the midst of the uncertainty, God makes us the same promise He made to Mary: "I will be with you." Is there an area of your life where God is asking you to follow Him into the unknown? How can Mary's example help you to obey without fear?

Quiet your heart and enjoy His presence. . . . He doesn't promise to reveal every detail of His plan for you, but He promises never to leave your side.

Not only does God promise never to leave us, He has given us a mother who is attentive to our every need. We can entrust ourselves to her care because there is nothing she wants more than to draw us to Jesus and to see us become more and more like Him.

Draw close to Jesus through Mary. . . .

Mary, I want to love and follow the Lord the way you did. Please intercede on my behalf. While I do all I can to remain like putty in the Lord's hands, please ask your Son to give me the grace I need to obey Him.

Hail Mary, full of grace; the Lord is with thee; blessed art thou among women, and blessed is the fruit of thy womb, Jesus. Holy Mary, Mother of God, pray for us sinners, now and at the hour of our death. Amen.

Day Two
MARY: PILLAR OF FAITH

"Now faith is the assurance of things hoped for, the conviction of things not seen." (Hebrews 11:1, RSV)

"The coming of faith first occurs in the Virgin's heart and then fruitfulness comes to the Mother's womb." —Saint Augustine

1. How did Elizabeth describe Mary in Luke 1:45?

2. A. Hebrews 11:1 tells us that faith is believing in what we cannot see. In John 11:40, what is promised to us if we believe?

   B. In what way did the promise of John 11:40 come true for Mary?

3. According to James 1:3, what does the testing of our faith produce?

4. Throughout her life, Mary persevered on her pilgrimage of faith. Each step of the way, she had to choose to trust God with the unknown. Edward Sri beautifully describes the culmination of this journey at the foot of the cross:

> At this crucial moment, however, no human crutch can support Mary. The only thing Mary can cling to is faith—faith that this is indeed the Son of God, who will reign forever; faith that she really is "the mother of my Lord" as Elizabeth told her; faith that this "sword" is truly part of God's plan as Simeon prophesied long ago, and that her son once again is doing his "Father's business." When Mary is found "standing by the cross of Jesus," she is, doubtless, experiencing great sorrow. But as a faithful disciple to the end, Mary also stands by the cross in great faith, trusting in God's plan for her son and clinging to what the Lord has revealed to her through angels, shepherds, prophets and Jesus himself.[27]

We all reach a point in life when all we can cling to is faith. We're at the bottom of our resources. We can't get ourselves out of whatever situation we are in. All we can do is trust that God will get us through. In what area of life do you need to trust God today? Write a prayer to Him, asking Him to increase your faith in His ability and willingness to take care of this concern. Ask Mary to intercede for you, to pray that you will persevere in faith so you can see God glorified in your circumstances.

Quiet your heart and enjoy His presence. . . . You will be blessed if you believe.

The fundamental attitude in the life of the Mother of God was one of faith. Mary trusted in God's Providence. As Elizabeth said of her: "Blessed is she who believed that there would be a fulfillment of what was spoken to her from the Lord" (Luke 1:45). I pray that your lives will likewise be marked by a deep faith in the providence of God. Then, with trusting surrender to the Lord's will in all things, you will be hope-filled witnesses of Christ in the world. May Mary obtain this grace for you. And may her divine Son bless you with his peace. —Saint John Paul II, Address to Marists, Rome, September 27, 1985

What has the Lord spoken to you? What has He promised? He has promised His presence. He has promised there is always a purpose in whatever you face. He has promised that He is in control. Can

---

[27] Ibid., 142.

you surrender to Him? Can you release your grip on your plans? Can you trust that His way is the best one, even if it seems to be a crooked path to follow? Ask Him for the gift of faith—for the belief in His power when you can't see it and His presence when you can't feel it.

Day Three
MARY: OUR LADY OF SORROWS

1. When Elizabeth greeted Mary and praised her faith (Luke 1:42–45), Mary responded with a psalm of praise. What were the first words of her song? See Luke 1:46–47.

2. After Jesus' birth, Mary and Joseph brought Him to the temple to present Him to the Lord. There they encountered Simeon, a prophet. What did he tell Mary her future held? See Luke 2:34–35.

3. When was Mary's heart "pierced with a sword"? See John 19:25.

4. Mary's soul magnified the Lord through her suffering, when her heart was pierced at the foot of the cross. Edward Sri issues us a challenge as we meditate on her suffering: "If we desire to magnify God in our souls, we too must be willing to draw near to Christ's cross and be pierced by the sword."[28] Do you agree? In what

---

28 Ibid., 103.

way have you seen God increase in importance in your life when you have drawn near to Him in suffering?

Quiet your heart and enjoy His presence. . . . Bring your suffering to the foot of the cross.

"Prayer to Our Lady of Lourdes"

O Holy Virgin, in the midst of your days of glory, do not forget the sorrows of this earth. Cast a merciful glance upon those who are suffering, struggling against difficulties, with their lips constantly pressed against life's bitter cup.
Have pity on those who love each other and are separated.
Have pity on our rebellious hearts.
Have pity on our weak faith.
Have pity on those we love.
Have pity on those who weep, on those who pray, on those who fear.
Grant hope and peace to all.
Amen. —Abbé Perreyve

Day Four
MARY: MOTHER OF MERCY

Saint John Paul II beautifully explains why we call Mary the Mother of Mercy in his encyclical titled *Rich in Mercy*:

> *No one has experienced, to the same degree as the Mother of the crucified One*, the mystery of the cross, the overwhelming encounter of divine transcendent justice with love: that "kiss" given by mercy to justice. No one has received into his heart, as much as Mary did, that mystery, that truly divine dimension of the Redemption effected on Calvary by means of the death of the Son, together with the sacrifice of her maternal heart, together with her definitive *"fiat."* Mary, then, is the one who *has the deepest knowledge of the mystery of God's mercy*. She knows its price, she knows how great it is. In this sense, we call her the *Mother of mercy*, our Lady of mercy, or Mother of divine mercy.[29]

---

[29] John Paul II, *Dives in Misericordia* (Rome: Libreria Editrice Vaticana, 1980), section 9, http://w2.vatican.va/content/john-paul-ii/en/encyclicals/documents/hf_jp-ii_enc_30111980_dives-in-misericordia.html.

1. How did the cross exemplify "justice with love: that 'kiss' given by mercy to justice"? Read the following verses and summarize.

   Romans 3:23–24

   Romans 6:23

   Romans 5:8

   2 Corinthians 5:21

   Summarize what you learned from these verses:

2. Read CCC 725. How are we described in this Catechism passage? According to this passage, what does the Holy Spirit do through Mary? Who does this passage say are the first to accept Christ?

3. Why is humility the precursor to accepting Christ? See Titus 3:4–5.

Quiet your heart and enjoy His presence. . . . Accept His kiss of mercy.

O Mary,
Mother of Mercy,
watch over all people,
that the cross of Christ
may not be emptied
of its power,
that man might not stray from
the path of the good
or become blind to sin,
but may put his hope
ever more fully in God,
who is "rich in mercy"
(Eph. 2:4).
may he carry out
the good works prepared
by God beforehand
(cf. Eph. 2:10)
and so live completely
"for the praise
of his glory"
(Eph. 1:12).
Veritatis Splendor, 120

Day Five
SAINT'S STORY

Saint Bernadette Soubirous

Bernadette was born in France in 1844 into a loving, successful family. During her early childhood, her family's fortunes turned, plunging them into dire poverty. Bernadette suffered from chronic illness, and due to her family's circumstances, she was not well educated. Her biography leaves nothing to suggest that she would become a great saint. But even as she lived in poverty, the Lord was close to her and working in her life.

When she was fourteen years old, Bernadette received her first vision of the Blessed Virgin Mary, whom she knew as "a beautiful lady." She would go on to receive eighteen such visions in a grotto on the outskirts of Lourdes, France. Her visions were widely doubted, and Bernadette paid dearly for the privilege of seeing Mary. The people mocked her, accused her, and made a great display of her.

But Bernadette learned from Mary that her heaven was within. She learned that even if she walked through a desert of scorn and misunderstanding, deep inside her was a well of joy, a river of healing that did not come from her but flowed through her—just like the healing stream that sprang up under her fingers at the grotto.

Through these visions, Bernadette also learned that God is good. He is not a faraway Father; He is Abba, Daddy, Papa: close at hand and full of tenderness. She saw the face of God shining through Mary's gentle eyes. She learned that God is not to be feared, but to be loved and trusted. In these visions, Mary taught her that prayer is an experience of being loved to the very roots of her being; she learned to approach God with all the confidence of a child who knows that she is loved, and whose Father will provide for her. God is beautiful, and He is the author of everything true, lovely, and good.

Bernadette never sought fame for her visions or with the knowledge she learned. But she did become a bit of a national spectacle, with people traveling to Lourdes to hear from her.

She eventually entered the convent at Nevers in 1866 to live a quiet life. Here, Bernadette (called Sister Marie Bernarde) lived simply, eschewing the fame of the world. She continued to suffer ill health for the next thirteen years, in addition to the skepticism of her superiors at the convent. Still, she never lost faith, and lived her life in devotion and service to the Lord and the Blessed Virgin. She let the lessons she learned completely take over her heart and fill her with holy love and service to others.

Most of all, she learned from her visions that God sees each one of us, no matter how insignificant we may be. We all have an important part in His plan. Bernadette was chosen to be His instrument at Lourdes, and she lived her life echoing the words of the Blessed Virgin: "He who is mighty has done great things for me, and holy is his name" (Luke 1:49).

True prayer is this constant gazing, this looking upon, this being with, this faithful contemplation of God's beauty and goodness. That is what Bernadette experienced. Saint Bernadette learned great lessons from Mary, which helped her during struggles in her life. Which of Mary's lessons would help you right now?

Conclusion

In Mary, we have a mother who will never leave us, one who is totally dedicated to our well-being. She knows that nothing will bring us greater fulfillment and satisfaction than being close to her Son. She "continues to intercede for her children, to be a model of faith and charity for all, and to exercise over [us] a salutary influence deriving from the superabundant merits of Christ" (*Compendium of the Catechism of the Catholic Church* 197).

Jesus, who held nothing back from us, offers us His mother. She is one of His most precious gifts, and He longs for us to know her, admire her, and become more like her. There's a love that only a mother can give, and He wants us to experience that love at its best.

Her "fiat," her yes, changed the world. Her life quietly reminds us that sacrificial love is the only love that really makes a difference. Loving with abandon can involve risk, the loss of reputation, and the letting go of a comfortable life. It isn't a safe love, but it's the kind that brings light to the darkness around us.

As Saint John Paul II said, "She, more than any creature, shows us that the perfection of love is the only goal that matters, that it alone is the measure of holiness and the way to perfect communion with the Father, the Son, and Holy Spirit."[30]

Nestle into your place in the family. Let Mother Mary love you, pray for you, and challenge you to love radically, sacrificially, and wholeheartedly. You are not an orphan. You belong; you are cherished. This family is the safe place to land, refuel, and then launch into a world that needs your yes. May your time "at home" give you the strength to hold nothing back, and to echo Mary's words, "May it be done to me according to your Word" (Luke 1:38).

My Resolution

In what specific way will I apply what I have learned in this lesson?

Examples:

1. I'll increase my devotion to Mary by praying a decade of the Rosary every night.

---

[30] Margaret R. Bunson, *Pope John Paul II's Book of Mary* (Huntington, IN: Our Sunday Visitor, 1996), 17.

2. To help me follow Mary's example, I'll take time this week to read the following words from Saint John Paul II and pray about areas where I need to improve: "In light of Mary, the Church sees in the face of women the reflection of a beauty which mirrors the loftiest sentiments of which the human heart is capable: the self-offering totality of love; the strength that is capable of bearing the greatest sorrows; limitless fidelity and tireless devotion to work; the ability to combine penetrating intuition with words of support and encouragement."[31]

3. When I hear God asking me to step out into unknown territory, I'll remember Mary's example as she responded to the angel, and I'll follow that example by saying yes to what He asks.

4. I'll take time this week to go to adoration, and when I'm there, I'll meditate on how the cross was the "kiss given by mercy to justice."

My resolution:

Catechism Clips

CCC 725 Finally, through Mary, the Holy Spirit begins to bring men, the objects of God's merciful love, *into communion* with Christ. And the humble are always the first to accept him: shepherds, magi, Simeon and Anna, the bride and groom at Cana, and the first disciples.

Compendium of the Catechism of the Catholic Church 100
In what way is the spiritual motherhood of Mary universal?
Mary had only one Son, Jesus, but in Him, her spiritual motherhood extends to all whom He came to save. Obediently standing at the side of the new Adam, Jesus Christ, the Virgin is the new Eve, the true mother of all the living, who with a mother's love cooperates in their birth and their formation in the order of grace. Virgin and Mother, Mary is the figure of the Church, its most perfect realization.

---

[31] Pope John Paul II, *The Mother of the Redeemer: Redemptoris Mater* (Washington, DC: United States Conference of Catholic Bishops, 1987), 51.

Compendium of the Catechism of the Catholic Church 197

How does the Virgin Mary help the Church?

After the Ascension of her Son, the Virgin Mary aided the beginnings of the Church with her prayers. Even after her Assumption into heaven, she continues to intercede for her children, to be a model of faith and charity for all, and to exercise over them a salutary influence deriving from the superabundant merits of Christ. The faithful see in Mary an image and an anticipation of the resurrection that awaits them, and they invoke her as an advocate, helper, benefactress, and mediatrix.

Lesson 5

SATURATED IN SCRIPTURE ~ WE NEED GOD'S WORD

Introduction

"Know this first of all, that there is no prophecy of scripture that is a matter of personal interpretation, for no prophecy ever came through human will; but rather human beings moved by the Holy Spirit spoke under the influence of God." (2 Peter 1:20–21)

"God is the author of Sacred Scripture because he inspired its human authors; he acts in them and by means of them. He thus gives assurance that their writings teach without error his saving truth." (CCC 136)

The Bible is unlike any other book you will ever read. It is the most popular, most powerful, and most precious book in existence. "No one really knows how many copies of the Bible have been printed, sold, or distributed. The Bible Society's attempt to calculate the number printed between 1816 and 1975 produced the figure of 2,458,000,000. A more recent survey, for the years up to 1992, put it closer to 6,000,000,000 in more than 2,000 languages and dialects. Whatever the precise figure, the Bible is by far the bestselling book of all time."[32]

The Bible is the most powerful book because it transforms, convicts, inspires, and teaches us. Within the pages of Scripture we can find the answers to life's most important questions: Why am I here? What is the purpose of my life? Why is there suffering in the world? What happens after I die? How can I get to heaven? It also addresses practical questions: What's my vocation? What qualities should I look for in a potential husband? How can I be a better friend? We can spend our lives wasting time, chasing after things that don't really matter in the end. We can allow the ever-shifting moral guidelines of our world to lead us, or we can turn to the truth found only in Scripture, and start building our lives on a solid foundation.

---

[32] Russell Ash, *The Top Ten of Everything 1997* (New York: Dorling Kindersley Publications, 1996), 112–13.

During this lesson, you will see an example of how precious the Bible was to Saint Irene and many others. This same appreciation for Scripture can be found today. Mark Hart, the executive vice president of Life Teen International, said, "How can we make time to read the daily papers or our e-mails and not God's love letter to us on a daily basis?" The Bible is God's truth, written in the form of a letter to us, His children. Although written by human hands, it was composed under the inspiration of the Holy Spirit, as if He were whispering in the ear of the writer.

How can we ignore such an amazing gift? In the words of Saint Jerome, "Ignorance of Scripture is Ignorance of Christ." He puts it pretty strongly! But he's right. If we want to really know Christ and move beyond a religion that's only in our heads to something that penetrates our hearts and changes us, we have to be willing to take the time to read the Bible.

Day One
IT'S WORTH READING BECAUSE IT'S TRUSTWORTHY

For a lot of us, it's hard to be enthusiastic about cracking open the Bible because we wonder whether it's relevant and true, or just a bunch of stories that are more mythical than historical. Can it be trusted?

This is an essential question to wrestle with, because two things are needed if reading the Bible is to really benefit us. First, we have to believe that what's written in it is reliable and true, and then we need to give the Bible's truths the chance to sink deep into our hearts and minds and impact our thoughts and behaviors.

1. What did you think about the Bible as you were growing up? Did you have doubts about its relevance or truth? Remember, this is the safe place to record your thoughts. There are no right or wrong answers to this question.

2. In order to embrace the Bible as truth, we have to believe that what we hold in our hands is an accurate version of what was originally written. Otherwise, it's as if we're the last person to be whispered to in the "telephone" game and the final message is mixed up.

The following chart compares respected historical texts. How often do you doubt the validity of Caesar's or Aristotle's writing? How do you feel the Bible measures up? Does this impact your opinion of the trustworthiness of Scripture?

Unparalleled Manuscript Support[33]				
Author	**When Written**	**Earliest Copy**	**Time Span**	**Number of Copies**
Caesar	100–44 BC	900 AD	1,000 years	10
Tacitus	100 AD	1100 AD	1,000 years	20
Suetonius	75–160 AD	950 AD	800 years	8
Herodotus	480–425 BC	900 AD	1,300 years	8
Aristotle	384–322 BC	1100 AD	1,400 years	49
New Testament	45–100 AD	Fragment: 125 AD; Full copies: 3rd and 4th centuries	Fragment: 25 years; Full copies: 200–300 years	24,000

3. Read the following supports for the trustworthiness of Scripture:

Archaeological Proof
There isn't room here to document the many archaeological discoveries that have shed light on the validity of the truths of Scripture. Nelson Glueck, a renowned archaeologist who uncovered more than fifteen hundred ancient sites during his lifetime, said, "No archaeological discovery has ever controverted [overturned] a Biblical reference. Scores of archaeological findings have been made which confirm in clear outline or in exact detail historical statements in the Bible. And, by the same token, proper evaluation of Biblical descriptions has often led to amazing discoveries."[34]

Eyewitness Support
Eyewitnesses were willing to die for the truths contained in the Gospels. Also, because the authors were alive while the letters of the New Testament were in circulation, there was plenty of opportunity for them to answer questions and defend their claims.

---

[33] Garry Poole and Judson Poling, *How Reliable Is the Bible?* (Grand Rapids, MI: Zondervan, 1998), 38.
[34] Nelson Glueck, *Rivers in the Desert: A History of the Negev* (New York: Farrar, Straus & Cudahy, 1959), 31.

Old Testament Prophecies
The Old Testament contains dozens of prophecies about Jesus that were fulfilled in the New Testament.

Cohesiveness of the Overall Message of the Bible
Considering that the Bible had more than forty authors from every walk of life, was written over fifteen hundred years, was written in three languages (Hebrew, Greek, and Aramaic), and contains many literary styles (poems, histories, prophecies, letters, parables), it is incredible that the overall message remains consistent and cohesive. From beginning to end, it is the story of the Father's unrelenting love for and pursuit of His unfaithful children, His plan to reconcile them to Himself, and His instructions on how to enter into and remain in a relationship with Him.

Unusual Truth Telling
You'd expect a book that's presenting a specific religion as the best choice to put a positive spin on the depictions of its leaders and main characters. In this, the Bible makes it clear that its purpose is to tell the truth, not to hide the dirty laundry. Much of what is written reflects poorly on God's chosen people. It depicts their sins, unfaithfulness, and shortcomings. The divisions within the Church are described. The Bible's focus is reality, not presenting a cleaned-up, winsome version of the story of God's people.

Does anything you read surprise you? Is there an area you would like to research more in order to be reassured of the reliability of the Bible?

4. What do the following verses say in terms of the trustworthiness of God's Word?

Isaiah 40:8

Mark 13:31

Quiet your heart and enjoy His presence. . . . God and His Word are utterly trustworthy.

Jesus:
"Do not think that I have come to abolish the law or the prophets. I have come not to abolish but to fulfill. Amen, I say to you, until heaven and earth pass away, not the smallest letter or the smallest part of a letter will pass from the law, until all things have taken place." (Matthew 5:17–18)

Two men on the road to Emmaus:
"Were not our hearts burning [within us] while [Jesus] spoke to us on the way and opened the scriptures to us?" (Luke 24:32)

Jesus Himself believed in the trustworthiness of the Sacred Scriptures. He came to fulfill them, quoted them often, used them as a weapon in spiritual battle, and always upheld their veracity. He wants you to embrace the Scriptures as truth, as a sure anchor for your soul.

After His Resurrection, Jesus came alongside two men in Luke 24 and "beginning with Moses and all the prophets, he interpreted to them what referred to him in all the scriptures." (Luke 24:27) He longs to do the same for you.

As you read the Bible, invite Jesus on the journey. Ask Him to speak to you through it.

Dear Lord,

I want to read the Bible in a way that transforms me. I long to have the experience that the men on the road to Emmaus had. I know this is totally different from approaching the Bible just as an academic pursuit. I want to read it to know you better. I want to read it to know myself better, and the ways in which I need to be changed. Help me as I look into this book of truth. When I doubt its trustworthiness, please help me believe. Give me the gift of faith, and never leave me alone as I seek to know you better through the pages of your Word. Amen.

Day Two
IT'S WORTH READING BECAUSE IT'S THE KEY TO SPIRITUAL MATURITY

1. In 2 Timothy 3:16–17 is a description of five ways in which Scripture is useful. List them here, then explain what role each could play in your own life.

    A. Scripture is useful for _____.

    B. Scripture is useful for _____.

    C. Scripture is useful for _____.

    D. Scripture is useful for _____.

    E. Scripture is useful for _____.

2. Read Hebrews 4:12. When we read that "the word of God is sharper than any two edged sword, penetrating even between soul and spirit, joints and marrow," it may remind us of a dissection experiment in high school. A more helpful way of looking at this passage is to picture a skilled swordsman whose sword finds the precise mark. The purpose of finding that precise mark is not to inflict injury; rather, it serves to pinpoint the place in our heart that needs correction, comfort, or God's grace.

    A. When we read something in the Bible that hits the mark in our hearts, what should be our response?

    B. Have you ever experienced this during a reading of Scripture at Mass, or when you're reading the Bible? Record your experience here.

3. There are certain things in our spiritual journeys that only God can do. Only He can soften our hearts so that we long to know Him. Only He can save us through His grace. But because of free will, there are some things that only *we* can do. Only we can choose to ask His forgiveness. Only we can choose to live the way He asks us to. Only we can choose to mature in our faith by reading *and applying* Scripture. He won't do these things for us. He never forces us to choose Him. He holds out the Bible and hopes that we will choose to read it. Whether or not we study it and apply its truths reveals a lot about how serious we are about maturing as Christians. What are the obstacles that get in the way of daily reading the Bible? What can you do to remove them?

Quiet your heart and enjoy His presence. . . . Let's choose maturity and growth.

"Brothers, I could not talk to you as spiritual people, but as fleshly people, as infants in Christ. I fed you milk, not solid food, because you were unable to take it. Indeed, you are still not able, even now, for you are still of the flesh. While there is jealousy and rivalry among you, are you not of the flesh, and behaving in an ordinary human way?" (1 Corinthians 3:1–3)

When Saint Paul wrote this to the Corinthian church, he was longing for them to grow up. It wasn't enough that they had been exposed to truth. They needed to choose to be transformed by it. There was so much "meat" Saint Paul was willing to feed them, but he found he had to keep giving them "milk" over and over.

If we're going to mature, then we need to respond to what we read in the Bible. We can grow as quickly or as slowly as we want to. Some of us compare our Bible knowledge to people who have grown up reading it and we feel like we're late to the party. We might think to ourselves, "I've wasted so much time!" "So many people seem to know more than I do!" We wonder if we're ever going to catch up.

Be assured, it doesn't matter when you start. What matters is how you respond to what God is revealing to you at this point. The rate at which you'll grow is up to you.

Dear Lord,

I want to build my relationship with you on a solid foundation. I don't want to skip over any of the basics that are essential to knowing and following you. At the same time, I don't want to hang out in spiritual diapers any longer than is necessary. I want to move upward in maturity! Give me the strength and the desire to put into practice what you reveal to me in the Bible. Help me to resist laziness. May I make growing more like you the highest priority in my life.

Day Three
IT'S WORTH READING BECAUSE IT GIVES DAILY GUIDANCE

"Your word is a lamp for my feet, a light for my path." (Psalm 119:105)

"The Church has always taught that because Christ is God as well as man, all of his words and actions as recorded in the Gospels are not merely edifying events from the past. Christ spoke and lived them with you in mind, so that they are alive and relevant and addressed to you and the circumstances of your life at every moment."[35] *—Father John Bartunek, LC*

What guidance do the following verses give you in the following situations?

1. When you are feeling afraid (Isaiah 43:1–4)

2. When you are grieving (John 11:25–26 and Psalm 139)

3. When you are facing a major decision (Proverbs 3:5–6)

4. When you are unsure of how best to parent your child (Deuteronomy 6:4–9)

---

[35] Bartunek, *The Better Part*, 10.

Quiet your heart and enjoy His presence. . . . Let His light fall on your path.

We all want our lives to matter. At the end of it all, we'll want to see that our choices were the right ones. So what should we do when we're confused about the right thing to do? We need to go to the source of truth. We need to go to the One who made us, who knows the future, and who knows the hidden pitfalls ahead. It was one of Jesus' greatest heartaches to see people He loved walking down the wrong path. He had this to say to them: "You are misled because you do not know the scriptures or the power of God" (Matthew 22:29). Interestingly, Jesus didn't hold them accountable just for what they did with what they knew. He held them accountable for the things they had been capable of learning. Their choice to not know the Scriptures or the power of God was just that—a choice.

We, too, are held accountable for how we respond to the truth that is available to us. For all our excuses, we have to admit, the Bible is accessible to us all. But we need to pick it up and read it. Good intentions don't mean much if they aren't translated into action.

Dear Lord,

It's just embarrassing when I think that I can spend hours on social media and Netflix, but I unashamedly say that I don't have time to read the Bible. I realize that I have time for whatever I consider to be most important. Help me to make the most of my time. Help me to carry a Bible with me so that I can turn to you when little pockets of time appear.

Day Four
IT'S MOST EFFECTIVE WHEN IT'S HIDDEN IN OUR HEARTS

"The tempter approached and said to him, 'If you are the Son of God, command that these stones become loaves of bread.' He said in reply, 'It is written: One does not live by bread alone, but by every word that comes forth from the mouth of God.'" (Matthew 4:3–4)

Jesus was able to respond to Satan's temptations because He knew God's truth. When He was under fire, He didn't have time to go find wisdom for the moment. It had to already be in His head. He had memorized Scripture, and found those words to be His most effective weapon in warding off temptation.

Do you ever feel tempted to just give in? To take the easy way when you know the hard way is right? Does discouragement ever nip at your heels and take you to a place of darkness? If you memorize Scripture, the Holy Spirit will be able to bring God's truth to your mind just when you need to fight back.

You may think of memorizing Scripture as an activity for the über-religious, not for the average Christian. A blogger at She Reads Truth (shereadstruth.com) described it this way: "Recalling Scripture isn't for the overachievers; it's for the homesick." It's for those of us who know that earth isn't our home—heaven is. It's for those of us who don't want to be tossed all over the place by our emotions and instead long to be grounded in truth.

But how do we do it? Never fear. There are easy techniques that can help us to store away God's words in our minds and hearts. Pick a few that work for you. *You can do it!*

Learning Through Repetition

Every time you sit down to pray and read your Bible, begin by reading the following memory verse. The more often you read it, the sooner it will be lodged in your memory. Be sure to read the reference as well; it comes in handy when you want to know where to find the verse in the Bible.

Unshaken Memory Verse:

"So whoever is in Christ is a new creation; the old things have passed away; behold, new things have come!" (2 Corinthians 5:17)

Learning Visually

Write the memory verse lightly *in pencil* in the space provided. Read the entire verse, including the reference. Choose one word and erase it well. Reread the entire verse, including the reference. Choose another word, and erase it well. Reread the entire verse, including the reference. Repeat this process until the whole verse has been erased and you are reciting it from memory.

Learning Electronically

Go to our website under Courses and save the *Unshaken* Memory Verse Image to your phone's lock screen so you can read these words throughout the day. Practice it every time you grab your phone.

Learning by Writing It Down

Grab a piece of paper and write your verse down twenty times.

Learning by Seeing It Everywhere

Write your verse down on index cards and leave them in places you often linger: the bathroom mirror, the car dashboard, the coffeepot, whatever works for you.

Learning Together

If you are doing this Walking with Purpose study in a small group, hold each other accountable and recite the memory verse together at the start and end of each lesson. If you are doing the study on your own, consider asking someone to hold you accountable by listening to you say your verse from memory each week.

Quiet your heart and enjoy His presence. . . . Saturate your mind with His truth.

"I have hidden your word in my heart that I might not sin against you." (Psalm 119:11)

"Take the sword of the Spirit, which is the word of God." (Ephesians 6:17)

Memorizing Scripture helps us on multiple levels. On the one hand, the Holy Spirit can bring one of the truths of the Bible to our mind just before we might make a wrong choice. It's like a little whisper reminding us of what we know is true, but there's power in it, because we know they are God's words. For example, in the midst of a conversation in which we aren't listening well, the Holy Spirit can bring to mind Proverbs 18:2: "Fools take no delight in understanding, but only in displaying what they think." This enables us to make a course correction immediately instead of looking back later with regret.

Memorized Scripture can also be used as a weapon in the spiritual life. When negative thoughts and lies run through our minds, we can take a Bible verse and use it as a weapon to kick out the lie and embrace the truth. Verses that speak of God's unconditional love and forgiveness and our new identity in Christ are especially powerful for this kind of battle. When we feel defeated and like we'll never change, when we falsely assume that God must be ready to give up on us, the Holy Spirit can remind us of 2 Corinthians 5:17: "If anyone is in Christ, [she] is a new creation. The old has gone. The new has come!"

Dear Lord,

Please renew my thinking so that I don't get defeated before I even begin, convincing myself that memorizing Scripture is only for the super spiritual. Help me to see myself through your eyes. You know that I am capable of so much more than I give myself credit for. This isn't because you see all my innate untapped abilities. It's because you know the difference it will make if I depend on you and let you do the work through me. So I come to you, aware of my weaknesses, but assured that "I can do all things through Christ who strengthens me" (Philippians 4:13).

Day Five
SAINT'S STORY

Saint Irene Keeps the Faith

The Bible is not like any other book. Well, maybe we should say it's not *just* like any other book. It was written by real human authors, who used their own writing style and imagination and wits, but it was written by them under the special inspiration of the Holy Spirit. It is a privileged fount of God's own revelation: "All scripture is inspired by God and useful for refuting error, for guiding people's lives and teaching them to be upright" (2 Timothy 3:16). Saint Thomas Aquinas, one of the most brilliant minds in the history of humanity, used to read the Gospels on his knees. The Church calls the Bible the "soul of theology." God speaks in a unique way through the Scriptures.

Saint Jerome, the great fourth-century scholar who translated the entire Bible into Latin (the language of the street in those days), explained it like this:

> I interpret as I should, following the command of Christ: "Search the Scriptures" (John 5:39), and "Seek and you shall find" (Matthew 7:7). Christ will not say to me what he said to the Jews: "You erred, not knowing the Scriptures and not knowing the power of God" (Matthew 22:29). For if, as Paul says, "Christ is the power of God and the wisdom of God" (1 Corinthians 1:24), and if the man who does not know Scripture does not know the power and wisdom of God, then *ignorance of Scripture is ignorance of Christ*.

That last sentence is actually quoted in Catechism 133.

All the saints have had a deep love for Scripture, even those who couldn't read. Some even died because they refused to show disrespect to the Bible by allowing others to desecrate it. Saint Irene was one of these.

In the year AD 303, the misguided Roman emperor Diocletian made it a capital crime to possess even a single page of the Christian Bible. He was trying to wipe out Christianity and reinvigorate the old pagan religions. Three sisters—Agape, Chionia, and Irene, all of whom are now recognized as saints—lived in Greece at the time. They happened to have some biblical texts in their possession, so they hid them away. Soon afterward, God permitted them to be arrested when they refused to eat meat that had been sacrificed to pagan gods. This was a common test used by the authorities to identify Christians. The three sisters were imprisoned and interrogated, but they wouldn't renounce their Christianity. They valiantly defended the faith even as the governor Dulcitius violently tried to make them abandon it. Agape and Chionia were burned at the stake, but Irene was kept in prison. They hoped her resolve would weaken after her sisters' gruesome martyrdom; it didn't.

Meanwhile, a search of their house uncovered the hidden Scriptures, and Irene was called again before the governor. Asked who had ordered her to keep the documents in direct defiance of the emperor's edict, she gave this brave testimony: "Almighty God, who has commanded us to love Him unto death. For that reason, we prefer to be burnt alive rather than give up the Holy Scriptures and betray Him. . . . They were hidden in the house, but we dared not produce them: we were in great trouble because we could no longer read them day and night as we had been accustomed to do." The governor was not exactly pleased with this firm faith, nor by her courageous spunk. He sent her to a house of prostitution to break her down. But even when she was exposed—naked and chained, but praying all the while—to the rough clientele, she miraculously remained unmolested. So the governor simply had her executed.

What love for God's Word those saintly young women showed! Since they loved Christ and they knew that He loved them, they revered and savored His love letters, the inspired books of the Bible.

Saint Irene hid her Bible to protect it. Our Bibles are often hidden, too, but not in order to protect them. More often it's because we know people would think we were weird if we carried them around.

How can the Bible become a greater priority in your life? Dusting off your Bible and keeping it by your side can feel a little risky. But whose opinion of you matters the most?

Conclusion

"Happy are those who do not follow the counsel of the wicked, nor go the way of sinners, nor sit in company with scoffers. Rather, the law of the Lord is their joy; God's law they study day and night. They are like a tree planted near streams of water, that yields its fruit in season; its leaves never wither; whatever they do prospers." (Psalm 1:1–3)

I doubt any of us set out to "follow the counsel of the wicked." But if we don't take the time to learn what is true, and if we don't develop our intellect and educate our conscience, we'll be influenced by whatever seems most convincing. We will be tossed here and there, and we will lack the inner peace that comes from knowing what our Creator wants from us.

One thing we know for sure is that God didn't give us the Bible so that we would become smarter sinners. He gave it to us so that we would apply what we're learning and become more and more like Him. The point is, we don't read the Bible as an academic pursuit, simply accumulating new facts. We read the Bible so that we can put into practice what we are learning. As we read Scripture, we can see ourselves in many of the characters. We recognize that sometimes we act like the people who are opposing Jesus: We want our own way more than His way; we want recognition and to be the favorite instead of wanting someone else to be honored; we value the wrong things. But the good news is that we won't remain in that mind-set. Jesus loves us so much that He won't allow us to stagnate in our spiritual growth. He wants us to grow deeper in Him and to be conformed to His image.

Think about the process you go through when you wake up in the morning. When you drag yourself into the bathroom and look in the mirror, what do you see? Let's just say it's not when we are at our best. So, we set out to make ourselves look better. We shower, brush our teeth, put on makeup, and brush our hair. When you look into the Bible and see yourself, the key is *not* to read it and say, "Hmmm . . . that's interesting!" and then do nothing about what you have read. That's like looking in the mirror in the morning and not bothering to brush your teeth and comb your hair. James 1:22 says, "But be doers of the word, and not just hearers, deceiving yourselves."

But the Bible doesn't just help us become more like Christ. I know of no other writings that give me more *comfort* than the Bible. When I am afraid, feeling misunderstood, grieving, angry, or weary, God speaks to me through His words in the Bible. So often I'll read the Psalms and think, "That's exactly how I feel!" Or I will read Jesus' words to His disciples and be reminded that I am not alone—that someone more powerful is in control, cares about me, and is watching over me. I know that the Bible is living and active. As I read Scripture, I have experienced the kind of peace that only comes from God, filling up my heart and calming me down. What other book can do all that? No other. Only the Bible is a love letter to me (and you!) from the Creator of the universe. What a gift.

My Resolution

Reflect on the time you spend with God each day. When can you set aside time to read the Bible? Can you schedule this into your daily or weekly routine?

In what specific way will I apply what I have learned in this lesson?

Examples:

1. I will incorporate Scripture reading into my morning prayer time. I will read one Psalm and one Proverb every day. This will correspond to the date: On the fifth day of the month, I'll read Psalm 5 and Proverbs 5. On the sixth day of the month, I'll read Psalm 6 and Proverbs 6, and so on.

2. All week, I will carry an index card with the *Unshaken* memory verse written on it. I'll read it many times a day and have it memorized by the end of the week.

3. I will keep track of the time I spend in one day online, and match that time the next day reading God's letters to me, the Bible.

My resolution:

Catechism Clips

CCC 133 The Church "forcefully and specifically exhorts all the Christian faithful . . . to learn 'the surpassing knowledge of Jesus Christ,' by frequent reading of the divine Scriptures. 'Ignorance of the Scriptures is ignorance of Christ.'"

CCC 136 God is the author of Sacred Scripture because he inspired its human authors; he acts in them and by means of them. He thus gives assurance that their writings teach without error his saving truth.

Lesson 6

NEVER ALONE ~ WE NEED OUR CHURCH

Introduction

In our individualistic culture, more and more people are questioning why they need the Church. When American Gen Xers were asked by the Barna Group[36] about the importance of attending church, 49 percent said it is "somewhat" or "very" important, and 51 percent said that it is "not too" or "not at all" important. The stats regarding millennials paint a grimmer picture. Only two out of ten think church attendance is important. There's no evidence of this trend shifting.

What has caused this change? At a time when women are outpacing men in college enrollment and completion,[37] many women are frustrated with what they perceive to be a limited role within the Church. Another cause is frustration with the way the Church relates to those experiencing same-sex attraction. Still others cite hypocrisy within the Church as a prime reason for their disinterest. They are tired of people saying one thing and doing another. For some, this has gone a step further: They have been hurt by the Church and have walked away because of it.

Others feel that everything they hear in the service lacks relevance to the rest of their lives. They have limited time, and they'd rather spend it somewhere else. In addition, we are impacted by the consumerist mind-set of the Western world—we want what we want, when we want it, how we want it. We don't have patience with an experience that irritates us ("I can't stand the music"), bores us ("The homily was too long and had nothing to do with my day-to-day challenges"), or offends us ("People here are out of touch with where people are at and are judgmental").

---

[36] The Barna Group, located in Ventura, CA, is widely considered to be a leading research organization focused on the intersection of faith and culture.

[37] Mark Hugo Lopez and Ana Gonzalez-Barrera, "Women's College Enrollment Gains Leave Men Behind," Pew Research Center, http://www.pewresearch.org/fact-tank/2014/03/06/womens-college-enrollment-gains-leave-men-behind/.

Looking around at Mass, we wonder where the people are who are our age or like us. While we wish they were beside us, we also understand why they aren't. We all have high standards for the place where we share our most valuable resource: our time. If people don't see the relevance of the Church, they aren't going to come. Guilt isn't an adequate motivator anymore.

It's interesting that at the heart of our coming together as the Church we find the Eucharist, which means "thanksgiving" in the original Greek. And perhaps it's that spirit of thanksgiving that's really missing in our analysis of the relevance of the Church today. A couple of years ago, I had the opportunity to travel into the rural countryside in Zambia. Our group was invited to go to church with the villagers. Halfway through the service, we realized that they were following the order of the Mass as well as they could, with no priest present. They were baptized Catholics, but they only had the privilege of a priest visiting once a year. The Eucharist and the other sacraments were considered precious gifts—they certainly didn't take them for granted. Hearing them speak about the celebration that occurred when the priest came annually made me ashamed of the countless times I took for granted what I had available back at home.

In this very moment, Catholics in other parts of the world are literally putting their lives at risk in order to come together and worship. It's similar to the time of the early Church when Christians were fed to lions, beheaded, and imprisoned because they followed Christ. And what was the result of followers of Christ being persecuted in this way? They turned the world upside down. In the words of Jon Tyson, author of *Sacred Roots: Why Church Still Matters in a Post-Religious Era*:

> The growth of the early church is arguably the most remarkable sociological movement in history. The numbers are staggering. In AD 40 there were roughly one thousand Christians in the Roman Empire, but by AD 350 there were almost 30 million. Remarkably, 53% of the population had converted to the Christian faith. What on earth could have compelled half an empire to convert? How could a Jewish political rebel, crucified on a Roman cross, become the Savior of the empire that killed him? The early church leaders didn't have the things we now consider essential for our faith to foster church growth. They didn't have fancy buildings and social media, no celebrity pastors or vision statements. Yet they loved and they served and they prayed and they blessed, and slowly, over hundreds of years, they brought the empire to its knees.[38]

---

[38] Barna and Jon Tyson, "Sacred Roots Outline," http://www.bibleresourcelink.com/frames/pdf/sacred-roots-outline.pdf.

Could it be that it is time for us to overcome our deeply ingrained consumer mentality? Instead of abandoning the Church when it frustrates us, are we being called by God to dig in deeper with commitment to the local parish? What can we do together that we cannot do alone? And what does the Church offer us that we cannot get in other places?

"Let us hold unswervingly to the hope we profess, for he who promised is faithful. And let us consider how we may spur one another on toward love and good deeds. Let us not give up meeting together, as some are in the habit of doing, but let us encourage one another." (Hebrews 10:23–25)

Day One
WE NEED TRUTH TO STAND ON

I remember well a restless period of my life when I was learning about many different philosophies and theological perspectives, finding that *all* of them could be quite convincing. I was easily tossed back and forth depending on who made the most sense to me at the time. Because of this, I lacked inner peace, and I hit a wall in terms of my spiritual growth. With time, I learned that Jesus didn't want me to feel frustrated in this way. It wasn't up to me to figure out who had cornered the market on truth. I could rest, knowing that God wanted me to discover the truth about Him. Jesus had left someone in charge, and I could count on the promise that God would always make sure that His truth was protected. Let's explore the passages of Scripture that brought me to that place of understanding.

Read Matthew 16:13–20.

1. How did Jesus describe Peter in this passage? What did He promise regarding the Church? What did He give to Peter?

2. What was Jesus entrusting to Peter when He gave him the keys to the kingdom? What does the phrase "the power to bind and loose" mean? See CCC 553.

We can gain additional insight into the meaning of "the keys of the kingdom" from Isaiah 22:15–22. In the Old Testament, when a person carried the keys that belonged to the King, he was given a special position of authority. In this reading in Isaiah, we read about a steward who had that authority but who did a bad job. He had been given this special position of authority, but he misused it. As a result, the position he had held wasn't removed, but the keys were given to a successor. As in Isaiah 22, Peter's position was designated not just for him but also for his successors. Some of those successors were less than perfect, to say the least. But in spite of fallible people leading the Church, God has protected the doctrine of the Catholic Church so that we can have a rock to cling to when the storms of our culture threaten to wash us away.

A powerful video encouraging Catholics to "come home" says it well:

> Jesus, Himself, laid the foundation for our faith when He said to Peter, the first pope, "You are rock, and upon this rock I will build my church." For over 2,000 years, we have had an unbroken line of shepherds guiding the Catholic Church with love and truth, in a confusing and hurting world. And in this world filled with chaos, hardship and pain, it's comforting to know that some things remain consistent, true, and strong, our Catholic faith, and the eternal love that God has for all creation.[39]

3. In John 18:37, Jesus said, "Everyone who belongs to the truth listens to my voice." The following commentary from Father John Bartunek sheds light on what being led by truth requires of us. Read his words and write down your reflections on whether you find it difficult to be led in this way.

> Whoever lets himself be led by what is true will be drawn into communion with Christ and will hear and heed God's ceaseless invitations to follow Him more closely. **But being led by truth requires humility.** It requires recognizing a higher authority than oneself: if I am obliged to discover, accept, and conform to what is objectively true (morally, physically, historically), then I am not autonomous; I am not the master of my universe; I am not God.
>
> That act of humility, which frees us from the enervating bonds of selfishness, is hard to make. Our fallen human nature tends toward pride, self-sufficiency, control, and dominance. To resist that tendency requires

---

[39] Catholics Come Home, "2000 Years of Faith: The Truth Behind Our 'Epic' Evangomercial," http://www.catholicscomehome.org/wp-content/uploads/2012/12/CCH-Epic-Factual-Documentation-20121.pdf.

courage. It takes courage to obey the truth and expose oneself to the burning love of God.[40]

Quiet your heart and enjoy His presence. . . . He is near to all who call upon Him in truth (Psalm 145:18).

"They exchanged the truth of God for a lie and revered and worshiped the creature rather than the creator." (Romans 1:25)

This exchanging of truth for a lie is so very subtle. It's a slippery slope—a gradual accepting of what the world says matters most. We don't worship creatures in the form of carved-stone idols, but we worship comfort, money, beauty, and prestige. And when we worship them by allowing them a place in our hearts that was meant for God alone, we start to believe all sorts of lies.

It takes a lot of humility and courage to ask the question, "God, where have I exchanged your truth for a lie? Where am I defining truth for myself instead of humbly accepting what you have said is right and wrong?" If there is a teaching of the Church that you find hard to accept, take some time to pray about it with a humble heart. Ask God to reveal to you if pride, self-sufficiency, or a desire for control is getting in the way of you obeying the truth.

Day Two
WE NEED GRACE TO STRENGTHEN US

1. How is Jesus (the Word) described in John 1:14? According to CCC 771, what part does the Church play in Jesus communicating this to the world?

---

[40] Bartunek, *The Better Part,* 977.

2. According to CCC 774, what are "the signs and instruments by which the Holy Spirit spreads the grace of Christ"? What role does the Church play in this?

Many of us feel especially close and connected to God when we are in nature. Whether it's the magnificence of the mountains or the ocean, or the quiet of the woods, there's something in the beauty of the outdoors that can draw our hearts to the One who created it all in a special way. For others it's the beauty of music or of art that causes the soul to soar toward heaven. Because God is omnipresent (He is everywhere), we can certainly experience His presence in countless places. But it is only in the Mass and in the tabernacle that we experience His presence not just spiritually, but physically as well. If you long to be strengthened, filled, and sustained by the grace of Christ, there is no better place to receive it than at the Mass.

3. Look up the following verse and Catechism Clips to explore how Christ is present both spiritually and physically at the Mass. Record any thoughts below.

Matthew 18:20

CCC 1548

CCC 1392

4. Saint Teresa of Calcutta said, "The Mass is the spiritual food that sustains me—without which I could not get through one single day or hour in my life." Has this ever been your experience?

Quiet your heart and enjoy His presence. . . . "Grace is nothing else but a certain beginning of glory in us." —Saint Thomas Aquinas

Are you feeling weak? In need of guidance? Do you feel discouraged? Do you need a reminder that you are loved? Jesus waits for you—longing to shower you with strength, wisdom, hope, and unconditional love. The most powerful way you can experience His grace and presence is in the Mass. He is present there, spiritually and physically.

"Do you want the Lord to give you many graces? Visit Him often. Do you want Him to give you few graces? Visit Him rarely. Do you want the devil to attack you? Visit Jesus rarely in the Blessed Sacrament. Do you want him to flee from you? Visit Jesus often. Do you want to conquer the devil? Take refuge often at the feet of Jesus. Do you want to be conquered by the devil? Forget about visiting Jesus. My dear ones, the visit to the Blessed Sacrament is an extremely necessary way to conquer the devil. Therefore, go often to visit Jesus and the devil will not come out victorious against you." — Saint John Bosco

Day Three
WE NEED EACH OTHER

1. What insights do the following verses give in terms of our innate need for connection and belonging?

    Genesis 2:18

    Ecclesiastes 4:9–12

2. What was the early Church doing when its members came together in community? See Acts 1:14, 2:42–47, and 4:32.

The early Christians loved in a way that was truly radical. It captured the attention and the hearts of an empire, and the world was changed. Jesus said His followers would be known by their fruits (Matthew 7:16), and they have been. That revolutionary kind of love has continued to be at the core of the Church's activities as the centuries have passed.

The Catholic Church started hospitals and orphanages, and is the largest charitable organization in the world.[41] More children have been educated by the Catholic school system than by any other scholarly or religious institution.[42] The Catholic Church has made significant contributions to science: Catholics developed the scientific method[43] and laws of evidence.[44] The Catholic Church created the university system.[45] She continues to defend the dignity of all human life and the importance of the family. Her extraordinary contributions to art and architecture have brought inspiration, beauty, and hope to the world for centuries.

Yet today, so many of us feel ashamed of our story. We don't know how to articulate the beauty of what the Church has contributed and continues to contribute to the world. Yes—the sexual scandals and corruption within the Church are a part of who we are. But it isn't our whole story.

Perhaps part of the problem lies in the fact that for too many of us, our experience of parish life is totally different from the experience of the early Christians. I know that many of their circumstances were completely unlike ours today, so there's little point in making those comparisons. But what made the early Christians stand out was their radical love. And that type of love is as needed today as it ever has been. I believe the outpouring of love, mercy, and practical help that the Church became known for is still active and strong today. What I believe is missing, however, is an experience of that revolutionary love on a personal level. Is this what people feel when they walk through the doors on an average Sunday at Mass? Think about the deep sense of community and belonging that the early Christians experienced. Think about their strong sense of family. Then think about this: That is our heritage. That is what we should be experiencing today. But far too many people walk through the doors to Mass, and walk out again at the end feeling unknown, unloved, unimportant. Will anyone notice whether or not they come next week?

---

[41] Catholics Come Home, "2000 Years of Faith."

[42] Center for Applied Research in the Apostolate, "Frequently Requested Church Statistics," http://cara.georgetown.edu/CARAServices/requestedchurchstats.html.

[43] New Advent, "Science and the Church," Kevin Knight, 2012, http://www.newadvent.org/cathen/13598b.htm.

[44] Thomas E. Woods Jr., *How the Catholic Church Built Western Civilization* (Washington, DC: Regenery Publishing, 2012), 187, 198, 201.

[45] New Advent, "Universities," Kevin Knight, 2012, http://www.newadvent.org/cathen/15188a.htm.

3. In Galatians 6:2, we're told to "bear one another's burdens, and thus fulfill the law of Christ." What do you think can be done in our parishes to create a community where people feel they belong to a family, that they matter—that their presence matters and this is the safe place to land?

Quiet your heart and enjoy His presence. . . . Let His love fill you and overflow into the lives of your brothers and sisters in Christ.

"Now you are Christ's body, and individually parts of it." (1 Corinthians 12:27)

We need one another. Just as the head needs the neck, the leg needs the hip, and the fingers need the hand, we do not do well cut off from the body. To live as a family—as the body of Christ—will take a conscious choice. We live in a highly individualistic society that encourages us to stand on our own two feet, to rely on no one, to be confident in our own strength. To participate in a faith community— "doing life together," as opposed to merely attending a religious service together—takes time and sacrifice. When we draw close to one another, we receive the comfort of another's presence, but we also see each other's faults a little more clearly. But that's what it means to be in a family.

Our family spans the globe and includes every race, the rich and the poor, the educated and the simple. We are diverse. We are full of complex differences. But what draws us together is a love for Jesus and for His body—the Church.

Spend some time talking to the Lord about how it feels to walk into your parish. Ask Him to open your eyes to ways in which you can be His hands and feet, bringing His warmth, His grace, His provision, and His love to the aching souls that come to Mass week after week. Ask Him to help you see people as He sees them. And ask for the courage to step out of your comfort zone to radically love those God has called to be your Church family.

"If the Church was a body composed of different members, it couldn't lack the noblest of all; it must have a Heart, and a Heart burning with love. *And I realized that* this love alone *was the true motive force which enabled the other members of the Church to act; if it ceased to function, the Apostles would forget to preach the gospel, the Martyrs would refuse to shed their blood.* Love, in fact, is the vocation which includes all others; it's a universe of its own, comprising all time and space—it's eternal!"[46] —Saint Thérèse of Lisieux*

---

[46] Thérèse of Lisieux, *Autobiography of a Saint*, trans. Ronald Knox (London: Harvill, 1958), 235.

Day Four
WE NEED TO GIVE BACK

When we look at church as a destination—a place that we *go*—we inadvertently develop the mind-set of a consumer. We go there to have our needs met. We go there to be filled. We go there to receive. That is *part* of what the Church does for us, but it is only a portion of the whole picture. The way in which needs are met in the Church is not only through receiving the sacraments. Needs are also met through the hands and hearts of God's people—through the ways in which we minister to one another. This means that each one of us has a part to play. When we were baptized, we were anointed as priests, prophets, and kings. Each one of us has a mission within the Church, and when we do not step up and do our part, the body of Christ suffers.

1. What does Saint Paul encourage us to do in Galatians 6:9–10? How does he suggest that we prioritize where we spend our time "giving back" to our needy world?

2. What problem does Jesus describe in Matthew 9:36–38?

3. Why are there so few "laborers in the fields"? There are all sorts of reasons that we give for standing on the sidelines instead of stepping in and getting our hands dirty in building up the Church. We can call them reasons, but sometimes they really are just excuses. Read the following excuses, and record any insights you gain from the corresponding Bible verses.

    A. "I have given up hope that this parish can change. My pastor/DRE/music minister [you fill in the blank] gets in the way."

    Ephesians 3:20 and Mark 11:22–23

B. "I'm not that good at anything. What do I have to offer?"

1 Corinthians 12:4–7

No one is overlooked. God gives these spiritual gifts to *each of His children*. When He handed out spiritual gifts, He did not skip you.

C. "I'm too busy. I don't have time."

Psalm 78:3–4

Matthew 10:8

Hebrews 12:15

D. "I'm too young. Who would listen to me anyway?"

1 Timothy 4:12

These are the charges that are given to us. This is what God is asking of us. Hand it on to the next generation. Freely give away what you have spiritually received. See to it that no one misses the grace of God. We hear these instructions, we nod our heads, but *far too many of us do nothing in response*.

I get it. We're busy. We're stressed out. We already have more on our plates than we can keep up with. But what if our schedules are filled up with things that aren't really going to matter in the long run? And by long run, I mean eternity. What if when we stand before God and explain to Him what we've done with the time and talent He's given us, we realize that we used it selfishly or for superficial pursuits?

I understand that so many of us feel we have nothing to offer. And I truly can relate to that feeling of inadequacy. I feel as if God is constantly asking me to do things that are far, far beyond my abilities. I look at the tasks, and I look at my limitations, and I recognize that I don't have what it takes. So if bringing renewal to the Church depended on our abilities, then I'd have to say, "Fair point—we can't do it." But it doesn't. God isn't so concerned with how skilled we are, but He's very concerned with how obedient we are. As has been wisely said, "God doesn't call the equipped. He equips the called." And make no mistake—He is calling you.

Quiet your heart and enjoy His presence. . . . He wants to fill you with all you need to step out.

God is pouring His Spirit and His grace into you, and that leaves you with a choice. You can turn your focus inward and be so glad for this spiritual awakening. You can become a "spiritual consumer" who is always looking for the next thing you need to feel spiritually "high." Or you can embrace the power of the word and. You can keep doing the things that help you grow spiritually and you can turn your focus outward. We aren't here to form a spiritual club, to be a part of a holy huddle. It's time to step out.

Where is God calling you? It doesn't need to be some big mission or project. Start small. Just be obedient and respond to the needs that God places in front of you. What is driving you crazy in your parish? Can you step in and be a part of the change that you want to see?

Go to the Lord in prayer. Offer Him your hands and feet. Commit to Him to stop focusing on your limitations and the barriers in your way. Fix your eyes instead on Him and on His immeasurable power.

Day Five
SAINT'S STORY

Saint Anysia Walks the Line

Every Christian should love the Church with the same heartbeats with which he or she loves Christ Himself. The Church is Christ's own mystical body, His bride, and the chosen instrument of salvation. Saint Paul calls it "God's household—that is, in the Church of the living God, pillar and support of the truth" (1 Timothy 3:15). The New Testament sums up Christ's entire mission by saying that "Christ loved the Church and sacrificed Himself for her" (Ephesians 5:25). And this is why so many saints and martyrs have preferred to suffer horrible persecution rather than cut themselves off from the Church. Saint Anysia was one of these.

Anysia was a Christian girl who grew up in the fourth century in Thessalonica, which is known as Macedonia today. She was just a girl when her parents died. She used her considerable inheritance to benefit the poor and destitute throughout the city, and she never lacked for friends because of it. But soon a cruel persecution broke out in the city. The governor ordered that no Christians would be allowed to worship, on pain of death, lest they displease the local pagan gods. Displaying incredible courage, Christians continued to gather in secret for Mass on Sundays, knowing that it was worth risking their bodies to save their souls.

Anysia was surprised and confronted by a city guard while on her way to one of these celebrations. He asked her (none too nicely) where she was going. She was frightened and made the sign of the cross on her forehead, and the guard seized her, demanding to know who she was and where she was going. She boldly answered, "I am a servant of Jesus Christ, and I am going to the Lord's assembly." The infuriated guard reacted violently and tried to drag her to the pagan sacrificial service instead, but she resisted, whereupon he drew his sword and killed her, right there in the street. Such, sometimes, are the risks of being a faithful member of the Catholic Church.

Even more than her courageous death, it is her words to the guard that are so striking. In her mind and heart, as she made her way to assist at Mass, she was thinking of that sacred celebration of worship as a gathering of the Lord's servants with their Lord. It was no empty formula for her, no dry and soulless duty, no mechanical obedience to a nonsensical Church ordinance; it was a living encounter with the risen Lord, together with all her brothers and sisters in Christ.

Anysia recognized that her faith was not just a "me-and-Jesus" type thing. She knew that being a Christian meant being part of a visible, structured body of believers. Being there, being an active member of the Church, meant more to Saint Anysia than life itself. She clearly recognized Christ's presence in and purpose for His Church.

Why do you think Anysia risked everything to worship with the body of believers? Does her determination and courage make you think about your own level of commitment to the Church?

Conclusion

I owe a great deal to a wise woman who told me the truth at a time when I really just wanted someone to feel sorry for me. I had been a disillusioned, disgruntled, confused Catholic for about ten years. The Catholic faith hadn't been explained to me in a way that really made sense, I had felt mistreated by Church leaders who were operating out of their own places of hurt and brokenness (not that I could really see that at the time), and week after week, I'd wonder why I was even bothering to go to Mass.

As I sat with this woman, sharing all my complaints, I finished off the litany with the strong statement, "I just *can't* worship God in the Catholic Church." I looked at her expectantly, waiting for her to nod her head in sympathetic agreement. She was, after all, a Protestant Bible study leader. Surely she would advise me to cut the ties and come back to a Church that would meet my needs a little better. Instead, she said this: "It sounds to me like this isn't so much a problem with the Catholic Church. It's a problem with you."

I was shocked. Where was the sympathy? Where was the soothing response? She thought the problem was with *me*?

She continued, "You can actually worship God wherever you are. There's nothing that can get in the way of that. If you want to see change in the Church, *be that change*." Then she got up and left.

That was a pivotal moment for me. I lifted up my head and started looking around at Sunday Mass. I wasn't the only one who was walking out the parish door still with burdens, still with questions, wondering if it even mattered if I went to church at all. And God began to whisper in my head. What if change could happen for just a small group of us? What if we got together and started creating a community that met our need to belong and helped us unpack the truths that the Catholic Church had protected all these centuries? What if, in our little sphere of influence, we could see change, transformation, and healing?

The failure to engage people at the pressure points of their lives has an enormous impact. We have got to meet people where they are and offer real-life solutions for today's challenges. The gates of hell will not prevail against the Church, but the goal of the Church cannot be just to survive. If we want the Church to thrive, then we have got to say yes when Jesus calls us to step out of our comfort zones. We need to be the change we want to see.

There is a price we pay when we don't shrink back from this call—when instead we say, "Here I am, Lord. Use me." There are times when we will doubt if God can possibly work through someone like us. There will be times of weariness. There will be barriers that make forward progress slow. But bit by bit, step by step, arm in arm, we can push back the darkness. We can bring Christ's light and hope to a world that desperately needs to know that there is more to this life than career success, financial security, and outward beauty. All of that could be gone in an instant. There is more—*Christ* is the more, and it's up to us to share that truth with the world.

When we determine to *be* the Church instead of simply *go to* church, a fire will be lit in our hearts that spreads from one soul to another. It will burn up our frustration, reveal the truth, and help those in need in a way that will not only change us, it will transform the world.

My Resolution

In what specific way will I apply what I have learned in this lesson?

Examples:

1. Instead of looking at my parish with a critical eye, I'll look for a specific opportunity to serve there. I'll recognize that I don't need to serve in a way that brings me accolades. In humility, I need to be willing to serve in whatever way is needed.

2. I may not have time that I can offer to a parish ministry, but I can always offer my love and warmth when I attend Mass. I will make an extra effort to smile at people as they come in, to give a compliment to someone as we walk out, and to thank my pastor for all he does to serve our parish.

3. If my parish doesn't have a Walking with Purpose Bible study, I will prayerfully consider whether God is calling me to gather with a small group of women to offer it.

My resolution:

Catechism Clips

CCC 553 Jesus entrusted a specific authority to Peter: "I will give you the keys of the kingdom of heaven, and whatever you bind on earth shall be bound in heaven, and whatever you loose on earth shall be loosed in heaven." The "power of the keys" designates authority to govern the house of God, which is the Church. Jesus, the Good Shepherd, confirmed this mandate after his Resurrection: "Feed my sheep." The power to "bind and loose" connotes the authority to absolve sins, to pronounce doctrinal judgments, and to make disciplinary decisions in the Church. Jesus entrusted this authority to the Church through the ministry of the apostles and in particular through the ministry of Peter, the only one to whom he specifically entrusted the keys of the kingdom.

CCC 771 "The one mediator, Christ, established and ever sustains here on earth his holy Church, the community of faith, hope, and charity, as a visible organization through which he communicates truth and grace to all men."

CCC 774 The seven sacraments are the signs and instruments by which the Holy Spirit spreads the grace of Christ the head throughout the Church which is his Body. The Church, then, both contains and communicates the invisible grace she signifies.

CCC 1392 What material food produces in our bodily life, Holy Communion wonderfully achieves in our spiritual life. Communion with the flesh of the risen Christ, a flesh "given life and giving life through the Holy Spirit," preserves, increases, and renews the life of grace received at Baptism. This growth in Christian life needs the nourishment of Eucharistic Communion, the bread for our pilgrimage until the moment of death, when it will be given to us as viaticum.

CCC 1548 In the ecclesial service of the ordained minister, it is Christ himself who is present in his Church as Head of his Body, Shepherd of his flock, high priest of the redemptive sacrifice, Teacher of Truth. This is what the Church means by saying that the priest, by virtue of the sacrament of Holy Orders, acts *in persona Christi Capitis*.

Appendices

Appendix 1
SAINT THÉRÈSE OF LISIEUX

Patron Saint of Walking with Purpose

Saint Thérèse of Lisieux was gifted with the ability to take the riches of our Catholic faith and explain them in a way that a child could imitate. The wisdom she gleaned from Scripture ignited a love in her heart for her Lord that was personal and transforming. The simplicity of the faith that she laid out in her writings is so completely Catholic that Pope Pius XII said, "She rediscovered the Gospel itself, the very heart of the Gospel."

Walking with Purpose is intended to be a means by which women can honestly share their spiritual struggles and embark on a journey that is refreshing to the soul. It was never intended to facilitate the deepest of intellectual study of Scripture. Instead, the focus has been to help women know Christ: to know His heart, to know His tenderness, to know His mercy, and to know His love. Our logo is a little flower, and that has meaning. When a woman begins to open her heart to God, it's like the opening of a little flower. It can easily be bruised or crushed, and it must be treated with the greatest of care. Our desire is to speak to women's hearts no matter where they are in life, baggage and all, and gently introduce truths that can change their lives.

Saint Thérèse of Lisieux, the little flower, called her doctrine "the little way of spiritual childhood," and it is based on complete and unshakable confidence in God's love for us. She was not introducing new truths. She spent countless hours reading Scripture and she shared what she found, emphasizing the importance of truths that had already been divinely revealed. We can learn so much from her:

> The good God would not inspire unattainable desires; I can, then, in spite of my littleness, aspire to sanctity. For me to become greater is impossible; I must put up with myself just as I am with all my imperfections. But I wish to find the way to go to Heaven by a very straight, short, completely new little way. We are in a century of inventions: now one does not even have to take the trouble to climb the steps of a stairway; in the homes of the rich, an elevator replaces them nicely. I, too, would like to find an elevator to lift me up to Jesus, for I

am too little to climb the rough stairway of perfection. So I have looked in the books of the saints for a sign of the elevator I long for, and I have read these words proceeding from the mouth of eternal Wisdom: "He that is a little one, let him turn to me" (Proverbs 9:16). So I came, knowing that I had found what I was seeking, and wanting to know, O my God, what You would do with the little one who would answer Your call, and this is what I found:

"As one whom the mother caresses, so will I comfort you. You shall be carried at the breasts and upon the knees they shall caress you" (Isaiah 66:12–13). Never have more tender words come to make my soul rejoice. The elevator which must raise me to the heavens is Your arms, O Jesus! For that I do not need to grow; on the contrary, I must necessarily remain small, become smaller and smaller. O my God, You have surpassed what I expected, and I want to sing Your mercies. (Saint Thérèse of the Infant Jesus, *Histoire d'une Ame: Manuscrits Autobiographiques* [Paris: Éditions du Seuil, 1998], 244.)

Appendix 2
CONVERSION OF HEART

The Catholic faith is full of beautiful traditions, rituals, and sacraments. As powerful as they are, it is possible for them to become mere habits in our lives, instead of experiences that draw us close to the heart of Christ. In the words of John Paul II, they can become acts of "hollow ritualism." We might receive our first Communion and the sacraments of confession and confirmation, yet never experience the interior conversion that opens the heart to a personal relationship with God.

Pope Benedict XVI has explained that the "door of faith" is opened at one's baptism, but we are called to open it again, walk through it, and rediscover and renew our relationship with Christ and His Church.[47]

So how do we do this? How do we walk through that door of faith so we can begin to experience the abundant life that God has planned for us?

GETTING PERSONAL

The word *conversion* means "the act of turning." This means that conversion involves a turning away from one thing and a turning toward another. When you haven't experienced conversion of heart, you are turned *toward* your own desires. You are the one in charge, and you do what you feel is right and best at any given moment. You may choose to do things that are very good for other people, but the distinction is that *you are choosing*. You are deciding. You are the one in control.

Imagine driving a car. You are sitting in the driver's seat, and your hands are on the steering wheel. You've welcomed Jesus into the passenger's seat, and have listened to His comments. But whether or not you follow His directions is really up to you. You may follow them or you may not, depending on what seems right to you.

When you experience interior conversion, you decide to turn, to get out of the driver's seat, move into the passenger's seat, and invite God to be the driver. Instead of seeing Him as an advice giver or someone nice to have around for the holidays, you give Him control of every aspect of your life.

More than likely, you don't find this easy to do. This is because of the universal struggle with pride. We want to be the ones in charge. We don't like to be in

---

[47] Pope Benedict XVI, *Apostolic Letter: Porta Fidei*, for the Indiction of the Year of Faith, October 11, 2011.

desperate need. We like to be the captains of our ships, charting our own courses. As William Ernest Henley wrote, "I am the master of my fate: I am the captain of my soul."

Conversion of heart isn't possible without humility. The first step is to recognize your desperate need of a savior. Romans 6:23 states that the "wages of sin is death." When you hear this, you might be tempted to justify your behavior, or compare yourself with others. You might think to yourself, "I'm not a murderer. I'm not as bad as this or that person. If someone were to put my good deeds and bad deeds on a scale, my good ones would outweigh the bad. So surely I am good enough? Surely I don't deserve death!" When this is your line of thought, you are missing a very important truth: Just one sin is enough to separate you from a holy God. Just one sin is enough for you to deserve death. Even your best efforts to do good fall short of what God has required in order for you to spend eternity with Him. Isaiah 64:6 says, "All our righteous acts are like filthy rags." If you come to God thinking that you are going to be accepted by Him based on your "good conduct," He will point out that your righteousness is nothing compared to His infinite holiness.

Saint Thérèse of Lisieux understood this well, and wrote, "In the evening of my life I shall appear before You with empty hands, for I do not ask You to count my works. All our justices are stained in Your eyes. I want therefore to clothe myself in Your own justice and receive from Your love the eternal possession of Yourself."[48]

She recognized that her works, her best efforts, wouldn't be enough to earn salvation. Salvation cannot be earned. It's a free gift. Saint Thérèse accepted this gift, and said that if her justices or righteous deeds were stained, then she wanted to clothe herself in Christ's own justice. We see this described in 2 Corinthians 5:21: "God made him who had no sin to be sin for us, so that in him we might become the righteousness of God."

How did God make Him who had no sin to be sin for you? This was foretold by the prophet Isaiah: "But he was pierced for our transgressions, he was crushed for our iniquities; the punishment that brought us peace was upon him, and by his wounds we are healed" (Isaiah 53:5).

Jesus accomplished this on the cross. Every sin committed, past, present, and future, was placed on Him. Now, *all the merits of Jesus can be yours*. He wants to fill your empty hands with His own virtues.

---

[48] Saint Thérèse of Lisieux, "Act of Oblation to Merciful Love," June 9, 1895.

But first, you need to recognize, just as Saint Thérèse did, that you are little. You are weak. You fail. You need forgiveness. You need a savior.

When you come before God in prayer and acknowledge these truths, He looks at your heart. He sees your desire to trust Him, to please Him, to obey Him. He says to you, "My precious child, you don't have to pay for your sins. My Son, Jesus, has already done that for you. He suffered, so that you wouldn't have to. I want to experience a relationship of intimacy with you. I forgive you.[49] Jesus came to set you free.[50] When you open your heart to me, you become a new creation![51] The old you has gone. The new you is here. If you will stay close to me, and journey by my side, you will begin to experience a transformation that brings joy and freedom.[52] I've been waiting to pour my gifts into your soul. Beloved daughter of mine, remain confident in me. I am your loving Father. Crawl into my lap. Trust me. Love me. I will take care of everything."

This is conversion of heart. This act of faith lifts the veil from your eyes and launches you into the richest and most satisfying life. You don't have to be sitting in church to do this. Don't let a minute pass before opening your heart to God and inviting Him to come dwell within you. Let Him sit in the driver's seat. Give Him the keys to your heart. Your life will never be the same again.

---

[49] "If we acknowledge our sins, he is faithful and just and will forgive our sins and cleanse us from every wrongdoing." 1 John 1:9

[50] "So if the Son makes you free, you will be free indeed." John 8:36

[51] "So whoever is in Christ is a new creation: the old things have passed away; behold, new things have come." 2 Corinthians 5:18

[52] "I will sprinkle clean water over you to make you clean; from all your impurities and from all your idols I will cleanse you. I will give you a new heart, and a new spirit I will put within you. I will remove the heart of stone from your flesh and give you a heart of flesh." Ezekiel 36:25–26

Appendix 3
CONFESSION BY THE NUMBERS

Reprinted with Permission from Faith & Family magazine

CONFESSION BY THE NUMBERS

Pope Benedict XVI is emphatic about confession. "The renewal of the Church in America depends on the renewal of the practice of penance and the growth in holiness which that sacrament both inspires and accomplishes," he said at Nationals Stadium in Washington, D.C.

Pope John Paul II was also emphatic. He spent his last years as Pope pleading for more confession. He made it one of the Church's two top priorities in 2001's "at the Beginning of the New Millennium." In 2002's Misericordia Dei he sought to correct abuses of it. In 2003's encyclical Ecclesia de Eucharistia, he used formal language to declare its necessity.

Pope Benedict XVI shares both John Paul's urgency and his compassionate love for the sacrament of mercy.

"The liberating power of this sacrament," Benedict told Americans, "in which our honest confession of sin is met by God's merciful word of pardon and peace, needs to be rediscovered and re-appropriated by every Catholic."

Use this guide to rediscover, and help others rediscover, this crucial sacrament.

2 SATURDAY AFTERNOONS

1. The Grateful Penitent
Here's a story from a Connecticut parish.
A nicely dressed man who looked anxious and upset walked into a church, squinted at the confessional, and couldn't tell if there was a priest in it or not. "Is there a priest in there?" he asked a woman. He didn't care what priest – he just needed a priest. Any priest.

"Yes," came the answer. He barely acknowledged the help, and hurriedly entered the confessional. After a few minutes he emerged, looking like a different person. Gone was the haunted expression on his face. Gone was the urgency and anxiety. He was a man set free.

He smiled at the person who had merely pointed out the obvious and said, "Thank you," with the gratitude of someone who had just been handed an antidote to rattlesnake poison.

2. The Ultimate Therapy
Here's a story from a California parish.
A teenage girl's whole character suddenly seemed to change. She was moody and preoccupied for weeks, so her parents took her to a counselor.

Therapy sometimes does wonders for people who suffer from mental anxiety. In this case, it didn't help. Their daughter had seasons of improvement, but always ended up back in her distracted unhappy state. This continued through college, and afterward.

By coincidence, the therapist met her outside near a Catholic church one rainy Saturday afternoon. Stepping out of the rain, they saw someone leaving the confessional.

The girl asked if she should go to confession, too. The therapist advised against it. She ducked in anyway. She emerged smiling, the first smile the therapist had ever seen on her young patient. The therapist noted that in the days, weeks, and months that followed,

the girl was no longer troubled with her old moodiness and unhappiness.

The therapist started to look into confession more, and she decided to enter the Church. Now, she counsels regular confession for all her Catholic patients.

9 CONFESSION PROMISES
According to the Catechism of the Catholic Church, confession gives you...

1. Pardon and mercy
"Those who approach the sacrament of penance obtain pardon from God's mercy for the offence committed against him." (1422)

2. Reconciliation
Confession reconciles us with the Church, with God, and helps us reconcile with others. (1424)

3. A Welcome from the Father
Comparing our journey to the story of the prodigal son, the Catechism calls confession "the first step in returning to the Father." (1423)

4. A second "Baptism"
We are first "converted" and become Christians at our baptism, but a second "conversion" is needed. Said St. Ambrose: "There are water and tears: the water of the baptism and the tears of repentance." (1428-9)

5. Interior change
Peace comes from a "radical reorientation of our whole life, a return, a conversion to God with all our heart, an end of sin, a turning away from evil." (1431)

6. A new heart
"The human heart is heavy and hardened," says the Catechism. "God must give man a new heart... It is in discovering the greatness of God's love that our heart is shaken by the horror and weight of sin." (1432)

The world tells us that sin owns us, and that we can never change. "The Holy Spirit has 'proved the world wrong about sin'" and it is "the Consoler who gives the human heart grace for repentance and conversion." (1433)

7. A just penance
The penance that a priest gives "must correspond as far as possible with the gravity and nature of the sins committed. It can consist of prayer, an offering, works of mercy, services of neighbor, voluntary self-denial, sacrifices, and above all the patient acceptance of the cross we must bear." (1460)

8. The strictest secrecy
"Every priest who hears confessions is found under very severe penalties to keep absolute secrecy regarding the sins that his penitents have confessed to him. He can make no use of the knowledge that confession gives him about penitents' lives." (1467) "It is a crime for a confessor in any way to betray a penitent by word or in any other manner or for any reason." (2490)

9. Strength for the battle
Confession improves us, offering "spiritual strength for the Christian battle." (1496) It's a rescue boat "after the shipwreck which is the loss of grace." (1446)

January/February 2009 - Faith & Family

7 THINGS EXPECTED FROM YOU IN CONFESSION

1. Be contrite

The Catechism calls contrition "sorrow of the soul and detestation for the sin committed, together with the resolution not to sin again." (1451)

Perfect contrition "arises from a love by which God is loved above all else." Imperfect contrition is "born of the consideration of sin's ugliness or the fear of eternal damnation." (1452-1453) Either works.

2. Examination of conscience

The Catechism says that the sacrament "ought to be prepared for by an examination of conscience made in the light of the word of God." (1454)

3. Disclosure of sin

A penitent "looks squarely at the sins he is guilty of, takes responsibility for them, and thereby opens himself again to God and the communion of the Church in order to make a new future possible." (1455)

4. Confession to a priest

"All mortal sins of which penitents after a diligent self-examination are conscious must be recounted by them in confession." (1456)

5. Confession before Communion

"After having attained the age of discretion each of the faithful is bound by an obligation faithfully to confess serious sins at least once a year. Anyone who is aware of having committed a mortal sin must not receive holy Communion, even if he experiences deep contrition, without having first received sacramental absolution, unless he has a grave reason for receiving Communion and there is no possibility of going to confession. Children must go to the sacrament of penance before receiving holy Communion for the first time." (1457)

6. Satisfaction

"One must do what is possible in order to repair the harm of sins (e.g., return stolen goods, restore the reputation of someone slandered, pay compensation for injuries)." (1459)

7. Penance

"Absolution takes away sins, but it does not remedy all the disorders sin has caused. Raised from sin, the sinner must still recover his full spiritual health by doing something more." (1459)

CONFESSION IN 6 STEPS

1. You always have the option to go to confession anonymously, that is, behind a screen. You may have the option of going to confession face-to-face only if the priest offers it.

2. After the priest greets you in the name of Christ, make the sign of the cross. He may choose to recite a reading from Scripture, after which you say: "Bless me, Father, for I have sinned. It has been (state how long) since my last confession. These are my sins."

3. Tell your sins simply and honestly to the priest. You might even want to discuss the circumstances and the root causes of your sins and ask the priest for advice or direction. However, avoid explanations that are really excuses or rationalizations for your sins. You are here to own up to what you have done. The best confessions are honest and to the point.

4. Listen to the advice the priest gives you and accept the penance from him. Then make an act of contrition for your sins.

5. The priest will then absolve you, using these words: "I absolve you from your sins, in the name of the Father and the Son and the Holy Spirit." Then he will dismiss you, sometimes with a prayer. You may respond by saying: "Thanks be to God."

6. Spend some time with Our Lord thanking and praising him for the gift of his mercy. Perform your penance as soon as possible – in the church, if you can. All heaven is rejoicing with you!

January/February 2009 - Faith & Family

6 WAYS TO EXAMINE YOUR CONSCIENCE

1. Look at your Life

Says the Catechism: "The reception of this sacrament ought to be prepared for by an examination of conscience made in the light of the word of God. The passage best suited to this can be found in the moral catechesis of the Gospels and the apostolic letters, such as the Sermon on the Mount [Matthew 5-7ff] and the apostolic teachings." (1454)

The Two Commandments of love

1. You shall love the Lord your God with all your heart, with all your soul, and with all your mind.
2. You shall love your neighbor as yourself.

The Golden Rule (Matthew 7:12)

Do to others as you would have them do to you.

The Beatitudes (Mathew 5:3-12)

Blessed are the poor in spirit, for theirs is the kingdom of heaven.
Blessed are they who mourn, for they will be comforted.
Blessed are the meek, for they will inherit the earth.
Blessed are the merciful, for they will be shown mercy.
Blessed are the pure in heart, for they will see God.
Blessed are the peacemakers, for they will be called children of God.
Blessed are those persecuted for righteousness' sake, for this is the kingdom of heaven.
Blessed are you when people revile you and persecute you and utter all kinds of evil against you falsely on my account.

Rejoice and be glad, for your reward will be great in heaven.

The Five Precepts of the Church

1. You shall attend Mass on Sundays and on holy days of obligation and remain free from work or activity that could impede the sanctification of such days.
2. You shall confess your sins at least once a year.
3. You shall receive the sacrament of Eucharist at least during the Easter season.
4. You shall observe the days of fasting and abstinence established by the Church.
5. You shall help to provide for the needs of the Church.

The Seven Capital Sins

1. Pride
2. Covetousness
3. Lust
4. Anger
5. Gluttony
6. Envy
7. Sloth

2. Look at your Love

Read 1 Corinthians 13:4-7. Ask of each word: "Is this me?"
"Love is patient, love is kind. It is not jealous, love is not pompous, it is not inflated, it is not rude, it does not seek its own interests, it is not quick-tempered, it does not brood over injury, it does not rejoice over wrongdoing but rejoices with the truth. It bears all things, believes all things, hopes all things, endures all things."

3. Look at Christ

Read Colossians 3:1-10. Ask, "Do I indulge these?"
"If then you were raised with Christ, seek what is above, where Christ is seated at the right hand of God...

"Put to death, then, the parts of you that are earthly: immorality, impurity, passion, evil desire, and the greed that is idolatry. Because of these the wrath of God is coming upon the disobedient. By these you too once conducted yourselves, when you lived in that way.

"But now you must put them all away: anger, fury, malice, slander, and obscene language out of your mouths. Stop lying to one another, since you have taken off the old self with its practices and have out on the new self, which is being renewed, for knowledge, in the image of its creator."

4. Look at your Relationships

1. **My relationship with God**
   - Am I generous in the way I live the precepts of the Church?
   - Did I skip Sunday Mass? Did I try to make the most of it, even if distracted? Did I tune it out and not try to tune back in?
   - Have I been "saying" my prayers instead of praying them?
   - Do I send God away and block him out of certain areas of my life – social life, leisure life, work life, studies, etc.?

2. **My relationship with others**
   - Am I generous in the way I live the Golden Rule?
   - Do I put myself at the service of others, or do I more or less use them?
   - Do I show my spouse love in words and actions? Do I respect my spouse enough to be honest?
   - How am I with my children? Am I careful about the example I set? Do I try to build their character, or is my discipline all reactive?
   - How am I with my friends? Do I always make things go my way?
     Do I go along with them, even in what is morally offensive? Do I initiate or participate in gossip?
   - How am I with my employer? Do I make the best use of my time? Do I treat my employer with gratitude for employing me?
   - How about my parents and others in my family? Do I honor them all with the respect they deserve?

3. **My relationship with myself**
   - Do I battle the seven capital sins?
   - Am I another person when I am alone? Am I another person in my thoughts? Do I think things about others I would never say? Or do I strive to live the Golden Rule, even in my heart?
   - Do I live my Christian principles when no one is watching? Online? At work? In what I read? In what I watch? In what I listen to? In the car?
   - Every Sunday I confess to faults "in what I have done and in what I have failed to do." What good have I failed to do?

5. Look at the 10 Commandments

6. Look at your Kids

21 QUESTIONS FOR KIDS

1. Did I pay attention at Mass? Have I fooled around at church?
2. Did I say my prayers every day?
3. Did I say mean things to my mom or dad?
4. Did I always say "thank you" to people?
5. Am I hard to get along with (during school, at Grandma's, at home)?
6. Did I do what my mom and dad told me to do? My teacher?
7. Was I lazy around the house? Did I do my chores?
8. Did I hurt other people's feelings by calling them bad names?
9. Have I started fights with my brothers and sisters at home?
10. Have I blamed other people for things I do? Did I get other people into trouble?

11. Do I hit people when I get mad?
12. Have I forgiven people, or am I holding a grudge?
13. Have I cheated or been unfair in games?
14. Did I refuse to play with someone for no good reason?
15. Was I lazy about my schoolwork?
16. Did I fail to do my homework?
17. Did I cheat in school?
18. Did I ever lie to my parents? My teachers? My friends?
19. Did I take anything that didn't belong to me?
20. Did I avoid medicine? Did I refuse to eat food I didn't like?
21. Did I watch, or look at, something I wasn't supposed to?

---

7 WAYS TO PROMOTE CONFESSION

1. Go regularly yourself.
Our example evangelizes more than we know; people notice. We also give the priest the shot of hope he needs to stay in the confessional each Saturday. (It doesn't hurt to thank him for being there.)

2. Bring your family – especially children and the elderly.
Confession can give children a place to unburden themselves without fear, a place to get kindly adult advice when they are worried about speaking to their parents. Many families make confession an outing, followed by ice cream or coffee.

3. Mention it to others.
We often think of confession as unmentionable. But there's no reason not to tell people that we've gone to confession. It's an appropriate answer to the question, "What did you do last weekend?" Also, when discussing plans, feel free to say: "I won't be able to make it until later, because I want to get to confession."

4. Learn more, and spread your knowledge.
There are many books and pamphlets on confession. Buy books for your parish's pamphlet rack, with your pastor's permission. Have some material on hand to give to others as the opportunity arises. Two good books: Father Richard Rego's *A Guide to Conscience*; Scott Hahn's *Lord, Have Mercy: The Healing Power of Confession*. The *National Catholic Register's* reader-friendly "How and Why to Go to Confession" is available at NCRegister.com for free. Click on Resources, and then on the How to Be a Catholic Guides.

5. Follow the Pope.
Pope Benedict XVI is an eloquent spokesman for confession. "How can one not recognize in our age...that confession must be rediscovered and proposed anew? How many people in difficulty seek the comfort and consolation of Christ! How many penitents find in confession the peace and joy that they sought for so long!" He also recommends the Divine Mercy devotion, which places a special emphasis on confession.

6. Children, use your power.
Kids have led their families into all sorts of healthy practices, from recycling to quitting smoking. Why not confession? When a girl asked Pope Benedict if she could take the initiative in leading her parents back to the sacraments, he told her: "With a daughter's respect and love, you could say to them: 'Dear Mommy, dear Daddy, it is so important for us all, even for you, to meet Jesus. This encounter enriches us. It is an important element in our lives. Let's find a little time together; we can find an opportunity. Perhaps there is also a possibility where Grandma lives.'"

7. Mention it as a kind of "excuse."
If someone invited you on a walk through the mud, you'd say, "No thanks, I don't want to have to clean my shoes and clothes." When someone begins to engage in denigrating gossip, or wants you to watch an objectionable movie, or suggests plans that make it impossible to go to Mass on Sunday, the same answer is available. "No thanks. I would have to figure out how to get to confession again before my regularly scheduled time!"

January/February 2009 - Faith & Family

10 COMMANDMENTS

1. I am the Lord your God. You shall not have strange gods before me.

- Does God's law come first in my major decisions? Are there other "gods" – money, security, power, people, etc. – in my life?
- Do I dabble with things that can harm my faith – such as the occult – out of curiosity?
- Have I received Communion in a state of mortal sin?
- Have I deliberately told a lie or withheld sins in confession?

2. You shall not take the name of the Lord your God in vain.

- Have I used God's name in vain either lightly or carelessly?
- Do I tell jokes that profane sacred things or insult sacred persons?

3. Remember to keep holy the Lord's Day.

- Have I deliberately missed Mass on Sundays or holy days of obligation?
- Do I indulge mental distractions during Mass?
- Have I tried to observe Sunday as a family day and a day of rest?
- Do I do needless work on Sunday?

4. Honor your father and your mother.

- Do I obey my parents?
- Do I honor them if I'm an adult?
- Have I neglected my duties to my spouse and children?
- Have I given my family good religious example?
- Do I try to bring peace into my home life?

5. You shall not kill.

- Have I had an abortion or encouraged or helped anyone to have an abortion?
- Have I engaged, in any way, in sins against human life such as artificial insemination or in vitro fertilization?
- Have I participated in or approved of euthanasia?
- Have I physically harmed anyone? Have I insulted them?
- Have I abused alcohol or drugs?
- Have I been angry or resentful? Have I harbored hatred in my heart?
- Have I mutilated myself through any form of sterilization?
- Have I encouraged or condoned sterilization?

6. You shall not commit adultery.

- Have I been faithful to my marriage vows in thought and action?
- Have I engaged in any sexual activity outside of marriage?
- Have I used any method of contraception or artificial birth control in my marriage?
- Have I been guilty of masturbation? Do I control my thoughts and imaginations? Do I indulge in pornography?
- Have I been guilty of any homosexual activity?

7. You shall not steal.

- Have I stolen what is not mine? Have I returned or made restitution for what I have stolen?
- Have I cheated anyone out of what is justly theirs, for example creditors, insurance companies, big corporations?
- Do I waste time at work, school, and/or home?
- Do I gamble excessively, thereby denying my family of their needs?
- Do I pay my debts promptly?

8. You shall not bear false witness against your neighbors.

- Have I lied? Have I gossiped? Do I speak badly of others behind their back?
- Am I sincere in my dealings with others? Am I critical, negative or uncharitable in my thoughts of others?
- Have I shared what should be kept confidential?
- Have I injured the reputation of others by slander?

9. You shall not desire your neighbor's wife.

- Have I consented to impure thoughts? Have I caused them by impure reading, pornography, movies, television, conversation, or curiosity?
- Have I behaved in an inappropriate way with members of the opposite sex: flirting, encouraging flirtation, etc.?
- Am I careful to dress modestly?

10. You shall not desire your neighbor's goods.

- Do I envy the families or possessions of others?
- Am I greedy or selfish? Are material possessions the purpose of my life?
- Do I share with the poor?

Answer Key

NOTES

Lesson 1, Day One

1. Jesus said that if anyone wanted to follow Him, he had to deny himself and pick up his cross daily.
2. Answers will vary.
3. Answers will vary.
4. If we are willing to lose our lives for Christ's sake, we will actually save our lives.

Lesson 1, Day Two

1. Jesus never promised that following Him would make our relationships more peaceful; in fact, He promised that it would often cause conflict and division.
2. We are supposed to love our parents and children. Jesus never contradicted Himself, and countless times in Scripture we are commanded to love sacrificially, in the same way He did. This verse tells us that our love for Jesus should be greater than our love for our parents and children.
3. **Ephesians 4:2** We are to be completely humble, gentle, and patient, bearing with one another in love.
   Ephesians 4:26 It's not a sin to be angry, but we are to make sure that in our anger, we aren't sinning. We are to resolve our conflicts right away, not letting the issues fester.
   Ephesians 4:29 We are to check our words, making sure that "no unwholesome talk is coming out of our mouths," but only words that are helpful for building others up according to their needs.
   Ephesians 4:32 We are to be kind and compassionate, forgiving each other.

Lesson 1, Day Three

1. We have a very real enemy, who seeks our destruction. He wants to take us out at the knees because he hates us and is afraid of what we can do through God's power.
2. The whole of man's history has been the story of our combat with the powers of evil. We find ourselves in the midst of this battle, struggling to do what is right, at great cost to ourselves and aided by God's grace.
3. We are called to be watchful, to stand firm in our faith, to be courageous and strong.
4. To stand firm in our faith, we need to pay attention to our conscience. Ignoring the prick of the conscience leads us to sin, which weakens us in battle. We live, grow, and persevere in our faith by nourishing it with the Word of God and begging the Lord to increase our faith. Faith needs to be working through charity (love in action), abounding in hope, and rooted in the faith of the Church.

Lesson 1, Day Four

1. Jesus said that unless we become like children, we won't enter the kingdom of heaven.
2. Faith in our own abilities rather than faith in what God can do; self-sufficiency; a desire or need for control; a lack of trust.
3. Answers will vary.

Lesson 2, Day One

1. **A.** Each family had to get a year-old, unblemished, male sheep or goat. On the fourteenth day of the month, they were to slaughter it during the evening twilight, and take some of its blood and put it on the doorposts and lintels of their homes. Then they were to eat its meat with unleavened bread and bitter herbs.
   B. John the Baptist called Jesus the Lamb of God, who takes away the sins of the world.

C. He gave them bread and told them to take it and eat it, that it was His body. Then He gave them a cup and told them it was His blood, shed for the forgiveness of sins. The Catholic Church has always taught that this was the institution of the sacrament of the Eucharist.

2. God rained down bread from heaven. It was called manna and was like "coriander seed, white, and it tasted like wafers made with honey" (Exodus 16:31).

3. They probably were confused, and it would have tested their trust in Jesus to be open to looking at things in a new way.

Lesson 2, Day Two

1. Jesus claimed to be the bread of life, saying that whoever came to Him would never hunger, and the one who would believe in Him wouldn't ever be thirsty. This made the people complain about Him, saying, "Isn't this just Jesus? A man just like you or me? We know his mom. We know his dad. How can he claim to have come down from heaven?"

2. Jesus said, "I am the bread of life." He talked about the manna that had given short-term sustenance to the Israelites, but reminded His listeners that everyone who ate the manna died. Jesus said that anyone who would eat the bread that comes down from heaven (Him) would not die. Whoever ate the bread (Him) would live forever. He said that the bread He was talking about was His flesh. The people argued after this, talking about how it would be impossible for Jesus to give them His flesh to eat.

3. Jesus said that unless they ate the flesh of the Son of Man and drank His blood, they wouldn't have life within them. He promised that whoever would eat His flesh and drink His blood would have eternal life. He said His flesh was true food, and His blood was true drink, and that whoever ate His flesh and drank His blood would remain in Him and live forever.

4. Many of His disciples returned to their former way of life and no longer accompanied Him.

Lesson 2, Day Three

1. This structure has persevered throughout the centuries: "the gathering, the liturgy of the Word, with readings, homily, and general intercessions; the liturgy of the Eucharist, with the presentation of the bread and wine, the consecratory thanksgiving, and communion" (CCC 1346).

2. One meaning of eating and drinking without "discerning the body" is receiving the Eucharist without really believing that you are in fact receiving the body and blood of Jesus. It also has to do with having respect for whom we are receiving—having confessed mortal sin and having prepared our hearts.

3. Answers will vary.

Lesson 2, Day Four

1. The principal fruit of receiving the Eucharist is an intimate union with Christ Jesus.

2. The Eucharist strengthens our charity (which is love) and wipes away our venial sins. When Jesus gives Himself to us in the Eucharist, He revives our love and enables us to break our disordered attachments to creatures and root ourselves in Him.

3. Answers will vary.

Lesson 3, Day One

1. The 9 Confession Promises are pardon and mercy, reconciliation, a welcome from the Father, a second "baptism," interior change, a new heart, a just penance, the strictest secrecy, and strength for the battle.

2. Answers will vary.

3. **Exodus 34:6** God's very character is grace and mercy. He has consistently been slow to anger and overflowing with love and faithfulness. It was true as far back as the Old Testament, and it's still true today.

   Isaiah 49:15 I'm imagining the strength, power, and steadfastness of a mother's love. Then I'm imagining something more faithful still. This is God's love for me, and He will never, ever forget me.

   Ephesians 2:4–5 God didn't wait for us to clean ourselves up before determining that we were worth dying for. When we were spiritually dead and hopeless, His love for us caused Him to send His Son, Jesus, to pay the price for our sins. Because of His grace, His unmerited favor, we have been offered mercy and made spiritually alive.

Lesson 3, Day Two

1. **A.** Sin aggravates you.
   B. Sin makes you aggravating.
   C. We need to say it.
   D. Confessing helps you know yourself.
   E. Confessing strengthens us.
2. Answers will vary.
3. **A.** Freedom means choices count.
   B. Confession makes you freer.
   C. Confession is a personal encounter with Christ.
   D. Confessing a mortal sin is required.
   E. Confession allows you to tidy "venial" messes in your house.
4. Answers will vary.

Lesson 3, Day Three

1. The whole power of the sacrament of penance consists in (is based on) restoring us to God's grace and joining us with Him in an intimate friendship.
2. In the beginning, God wanted an intimate relationship with His children. This is what was experienced in the Garden of Eden when Adam and Eve looked at God and walked with Him. Everything changed when sin entered the world. Shame filled their hearts, and they hid their faces from God.
3. Answers will vary.

Lesson 3, Day Four

1. We become enslaved to sin.
2. We receive an increase in spiritual strength for the Christian battle.
3. Where the Spirit of the Lord is, there is freedom.

Lesson 4, Day One

1. **A.** He calls her "favored one."
   B. We are given saving, transforming grace. We're given redemption by Christ's blood, and forgiveness because of the rich grace God has lavished on us.
2. In Luke 1:28, the angel Gabriel told Mary that God was with her. Because of God's promised presence, she was told to not be afraid. Throughout Scripture, whenever God called someone to a great mission—one that would require courage and faith—the assurance He gave them was always *His presence*. He rarely gave the plan. Instead, He gave this promise.
3. She said, "I am the handmaid of the Lord. May it be done to me according to your word."
4. Answers will vary.

Lesson 4, Day Two

1. Elizabeth described Mary as being blessed because she believed that what was spoken to her would be fulfilled.
2. **A.** John 11:40 promises that if we believe, we'll see the glory of God.
   B. Mary believed in what the angel said, and clung to that truth even when it appeared that everything was spinning out of control. Because she believed, she was able to see Jesus resurrected from the dead, full of glory. She is able to see Him now, honored in heaven, sitting at the right hand of God. There were certainly times when she couldn't understand why God was allowing what He did, but in the end, she was able to see the beautiful tapestry that He was weaving—our salvation.
3. The testing of our faith produces perseverance.
4. Answers will vary.

Lesson 4, Day Three

1. She said, "My soul proclaims the greatness of the Lord; my spirit rejoices in God my savior." Some translations say, "My soul magnifies the Lord."
2. Simeon prophesied that Jesus was "destined for the fall and rise of many in Israel" and that a sword would pierce Mary's heart.
3. Her heart was pierced when she saw her Son suffering and dying on the cross.
4. Answers will vary.

Lesson 4, Day Four

1. **Romans 3:23** All have sinned and fall short of the glory of God.
   Romans 6:23 The wages (or consequences) of sin is death, but the gift of God is eternal life in Christ Jesus.
   Romans 5:8 God proved His love for us in this: While we were still sinners, Christ died for us.
   2 Corinthians 5:21 Our sins were placed on Christ—He became sin for us—so that in exchange, He could give us His righteousness.
   The consequence of sin is death. Death is what is due each one of us, because we all are sinners. Justice required that a death occur in payment for sin. Justice was satisfied when Christ paid the price for our sins. All our sins were placed on Him, and He died for us. In doing so, He showed us total mercy, because we didn't deserve this help. There is nothing we have done to earn the gift of our salvation.
2. We are described as "the objects of God's merciful love." Through Mary, the Holy Spirit begins to bring men into communion with Christ. The humble are the first to accept Him.
3. We have to recognize that we need mercy, that we need forgiveness, that we are sinful. We aren't saved because of any righteous deeds we have done, but simply because of God's mercy. If we don't recognize this, we'll try to save ourselves, and in doing so, consciously or unconsciously, we'll reject Christ's offer to pay the price for us. And only His sacrifice will satisfy God the Father.

Lesson 5, Day One

1. Answers will vary.
2. Answers will vary.
3. Answers will vary.
4. **Isaiah 40:8** Grass withers and flowers wilt, but God's words will stand forever.
   Mark 13:31 Heaven and earth will pass away, but God's words will not.

Lesson 5, Day Two

1. **A.** Scripture is useful for **teaching**. It can teach us that we know God's truth and His will for our lives. It can teach us about His character, which will help us to trust Him.
   B. Scripture is useful for **rebuking**. It can rebuke us by making it really clear what God expects. We compare ourselves to His ideal (which is always shown to us so that we can be fulfilled and happy) and we see where we're missing the mark.
   C. Scripture is useful for **correcting**. It can help us correct our motives, attitudes, and behaviors.
   D. Scripture is useful for **training in righteousness**. Jesus wants us to be trained in righteousness because He knows that many people will never read the Bible; they will read our lives. Our lives should reflect Him. We should look like Him. But this is a training *process*. It's not instant. It requires us to get back up and try again when we fail.
   E. Scripture is useful for **equipping us for every good work**. When God created us, He created us with a purpose. There are specific works that He wants us to do, and He only calls us to do things that He equips us for. Many of the tools we need to answer and live out that call are found in Scripture.
2. **A.** We should respond by obeying what we've read.
   B. Answers will vary.
3. Answers will vary.

Lesson 5, Day Three

1. Answers will vary.
2. Answers will vary.
3. Answers will vary.
4. Answers will vary.

Lesson 6, Day One

1. Jesus described Peter as the rock on whom He would build the Church. Jesus promised that the gates of Hades would not prevail against the Church. He gave Peter the keys to the kingdom of heaven.
2. When Jesus gave Peter the keys to the kingdom, He was entrusting him with a specific authority. The "power of the keys" designates authority to govern the house of God, which is the Church. The power to "bind and loose" means the authority to absolve sins, to pronounce doctrinal judgments, and to make disciplinary decisions in the Church.
3. Answers will vary.

Lesson 6, Day Two

1. In John 1:14, Jesus is described as "full of grace and truth." The Church, as a community of faith, hope, and charity, is the visible organization through which Jesus communicates His truth and grace.
2. The seven sacraments are the signs and instruments by which the Holy Spirit spreads the grace of Christ. We receive the sacraments through the Church. Without the Church, we wouldn't have access to the sacraments.
3. **Matthew 18:20** Where two or three are gathered in Christ's name, Christ is there in the midst of them.
   CCC 1548 Christ is present in a sacramental way through the person of the priest. This is what is meant by the phrase *in persona Christi*.

123

CCC 1392 Christ is present in the Eucharist. What material food does for us physically, the Eucharist does for us spiritually. In it, we are communing with the actual flesh of the risen Christ. This preserves, increases, and renews the life of grace that we receive at baptism.

4. Answers will vary.

Lesson 6, Day Three

1. **Genesis 2:18** One of the first things God said to man was, "It is not good for the man to be alone."
   Ecclesiastes 4:9–12 Two are better than one. If one falls, the other can help him up. One alone can be overcome, but two together can easily resist. And a cord of three is not easily broken.
2. They devoted themselves with one accord to prayer, to the teaching of the apostles, to living a communal life, and to the breaking of the bread. They shared all their possessions—selling property and possessions and then dividing the proceeds among themselves. They met together in the temple area every day. They were of one heart and mind.
3. Answers will vary.

Lesson 6, Day Four

1. He tells us not to grow weary in doing good, because in due time we will reap a harvest if we don't give up. We are to continue to do good to all, but especially to those who belong to the family of the faith. This indicates that our highest priority should be to give back to "the family of the faith."
2. Jesus was moved to pity when He looked at the crowds of people, because they were troubled and abandoned, like sheep without a shepherd. He observed that the harvest was abundant—the problem wasn't that people weren't open or interested in being helped; the problem was that there were so few laborers who were willing to go out and do the work in the fields.
3. **A.** We serve a God who is able to do immeasurably more than all we can ask or imagine. The same power that raised Jesus from the dead is within us. Mountains can be moved. Barriers can come down. We are not weak and powerless to bring change.
   B. The Holy Spirit is given to each individual child of God, equipping him or her with spiritual gifts that God wants him or her to use for the benefit of the Church.
   C. **Psalm 78:3–4** We are to pass on our faith to the next generation.
   Matthew 10:8 What we've been given freely, we are to give away, not hoard it for ourselves.
   Hebrews 12:15 We are to see to it that no one misses the grace of God.

Prayer Pages

NOTES

walking with purpose

Dear God,

Thank you for being at work in me, giving me the desire and the power to do what pleases You.[53] I'm grateful for Your guidance, and that I can trust that Your plans for me are for my good and not for harm, to give me a future and a hope.[54] Please show me the way of life—the right choices to make—so that I have the joy of being in Your presence and the pleasure of living with You forever.[55] The enemy of my soul wants to steal, kill and destroy everything good in my life. But Your purpose and plan is to give me a rich and satisfying life of abundance.[56] Help me to remember that even when my circumstances are hard, You are always at work, causing everything to come together for my good.[57] May I see myself as Your masterpiece—Your beloved daughter—created anew in Christ so that I can do the good things You planned for me long ago.[58] To You be the glory—You who are able, through Your mighty power at work in me, to accomplish infinitely more than I can ask or imagine.[59]

Amen.

---

[53] Philippians 2:13

[54] Jeremiah 29:11

[55] Psalm 16:11

[56] John 10:10

[57] Romans 8:28

[58] Ephesians 2:10

[59] Ephesians 3:20

Prayer Requests

Date:

Date:

Prayer Requests

Date:

Date:

Prayer Requests

Date:

Date:

Prayer Requests

Date:

Date:

Prayer Requests

Date:

Donation Information

Walking with Purpose expands when women in parishes respond to the inspiration of the Holy Spirit and step forward to serve their neighbors and friends through this ministry. As the ministry grows, so do the material needs of the Walking with Purpose organization. If you would like to contribute to Walking with Purpose, donations can be mailed to:

Walking with Purpose
15 E. Putnam Avenue
Greenwich, CT 06830

You can also donate online at www.walkingwithpurpose.com.
Walking with Purpose is a 501(c)(3) nonprofit organization.
Your gift is fully tax deductible.

"See to it that no one misses the grace of God" **Hebrews 12:15**

It's time to stop talking about how there's nothing relevant out there for Catholic women.

IT'S TIME TO BE THE CHANGE WE WANT TO SEE.

You can bring **Walking with Purpose** to your parish!

IT'S EASY TO DO!

- **You've already got the skills needed!**
  - Personal commitment to Christ
  - Desire to share the love of Christ
  - Belief in the power of authentic, transparent community

- **We'll be there every step of the way, offering:**
  - Training
  - Mentoring
  - Bible study materials
  - Promotional materials

- **Do you think you have too many limitations to serve in this way?**

Great! That's *exactly* where God wants us to start. If we will just offer Him *what we have*, He promises to do the rest. Few things stretch and grow our faith like stepping out and asking God to work through us. Say *YES*, and get ready to watch what He can do through imperfect women who depend on Him.

Learn more about bringing **Walking with Purpose** to your parish!

Visit us at **walkingwithpurpose.com**

walking with purpose

"For to the one who has, more will be given"
Matthew 13:12

THANK YOU

for sharing this journey with all of us at **Walking with Purpose**.
We'd love to stay connected!
We've got more encouragement and hope available for you!

FREE valuable resources:

- Print out or download WWP Scripture Verses, can also be used as lock screens for phones.

- Join our community on Facebook, Twitter, Pinterest and Instagram for a daily boost!

- Subscribe to our Blog for regular inspiration and participate in conversations by contributing your comments!

The Walking with Purpose Bible study program is
just the beginning.

Go to **walkingwithpurpose.com** to subscribe to
our Blog and connect with us on Social Media

walking with purpose

THE OPENING YOUR HEART SERIES

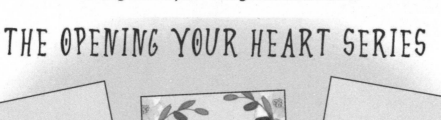

Beloved: *Opening Your Heart, Part I,* is a six-lesson Bible study that lays a strong foundation for our true identity as beloved daughters of God.

Unshaken: *Opening Your Heart, Part II,* is a six-lesson Bible study that fills our spiritual toolbox with exactly what we need to grow stronger in our faith.

Steadfast: *Opening Your Heart, Part III,* a six-lesson Bible study, unpacks why we are hustling for our worth and how to conquer our fears.

THE KEEPING IN BALANCE SERIES

Harmony: Keeping in Balance, Part I
Perspective: Keeping in Balance, Part II
Exhale: Keeping in Balance, Part III

THE DISCOVERING OUR DIGNITY SERIES

Tapestry: Discovering Our Dignity, Part I
Legacy: Discovering our Dignity, Part II
Heritage: Discovering Our Dignity, Part III

For more information on all Walking with Purpose Bible studies please visit us at **walkingwithpurpose.com**

walking with purpose

So whoever is in Christ is a NEW CREATION The OLD things HAVE PASSED Away. Behold NEW THINGS Have COME.

2 CORINTHIANS 5:17

walking with purpose